Hamlyn nature guides

Minerals

Hamlyn nature guides
Minerals
Andrew Clark

Hamlyn
London · New York · Sydney · Toronto

Acknowledgements

Ardea Photographics – P. J. Green 20L, 21L; F. B. Atkins – 88L; R. Böck – 112L; Herve Chaumenton – 41L, 47R, 51L, 67L, 88R, 90L, 99L, 103L, 110R, 112R, 114R, 116L, 117L, 123R, 124L; A. W. Curtis – 27L, 32R, 56L, 72R, 81R, 98R; Adrian Davies – 109L; Hamlyn Group Picture Library – back jacket, 87L, 111R, 115L; Imitor Ltd. – 16L, 109R, 111L; Jacana – 19L, 59L, 93L, 110L, 113R; Breck P. Kent – front jacket, title spread, 16R, 17L, 18L, 20R, 21R, 23L, 23R, 24L, 26R, 28L, 28R, 29L, 29R, 32L, 36R, 37L, 38L, 38R, 39L, 41R, 45L, 48R, 55L, 55R, 57L, 57R, 58L, 58R, 60R, 61R, 62R, 64R, 66L, 66R, 72L, 73R, 75L, 75R, 76L, 76R; 77L, 77R, 79L, 81L, 82R, 84R, 86L, 89R, 91L, 92R, 94L, 97L, 98L, 100L, 104R, 105L, 113L, 119L, 119R, 121R, 122R, 125L; I. Patterson – 18R, 19R, 22L, 24R, 25L, 25R, 26L, 27R, 30L, 31L, 31R, 33L, 33R, 34L, 35L, 36L, 37R, 39R, 40L, 40R, 42L, 42R, 43L, 44L, 44R, 45R, 46L, 46R, 47L, 48L, 49L, 49R, 50L, 50R, 51R, 52L, 52L, 53L, 53R, 54L, 56R, 59R, 60L, 62L, 63L, 63R, 64L, 65L, 65R, 67R, 68L, 69L, 70L, 70R, 71L, 71R, 73L, 74L, 74R, 75R, 78L, 78R, 80R, 82L, 84L, 85L, 85R, 86R, 87R, 89L, 90R, 91R, 92L, 93R, 94R, 95R, 96L, 96R, 97R, 99R, 100R, 101L, 101R, 102L, 102R, 103R, 106R, 107L, 107R, 108L, 108R, 115R, 116R, 117R, 118R, 120L, 120R, 122L, 124R, 125R; J. C. Revy – 43R, 61L, 69L, 80L, 105R, 106L, 123L; RIDA Photo Library – David Bayliss – 22R; R. Symes – 54R; Z.E.F.A. – W. F. Davidson – 52R.

The following photographs are reproduced by courtesy of the Smithsonian Institution, Washington, D.C.; front jacket, title spread, 18L, 23L, 28L, 29L, 32L, 48L, 57L, 58L, 58R, 72L, 75L, 76L, 76R, 77L, 77R, 79L, 91L, 92R, 94L, 100L.

The following photographs are N.E.R.C. copyright and are reproduced by permission of the Director, Institute of Geological Sciences, London: 17R, 30R, 34R, 35R, 68R, 79R, 83L, 83R, 104L, 114L, 118L, 121L.

The photographs taken by I. Patterson are reproduced from the private collection of Dr. R. J. King, Leicester.

Front jacket: mimetite.
Back jacket: stibnite.
Title spread: wulfenite.

Line drawings by Valerie Jones

Published by The Hamlyn Publishing Group Limited
London · New York · Sydney · Toronto
Astronaut House, Feltham, Middlesex, England
Copyright © The Hamlyn Publishing Group Limited 1979

ISBN 0 600 36313 9

Phototypeset by Tradespools Limited, Frome, Somerset.
Printed in Italy

Contents

Introduction
Chemistry and structure

Minerals are the naturally occurring chemical compounds from which all rocks are formed. Their compositions can usually be expressed by formulae indicating the elements present (Table I) and the proportions in which they are combined. A chemical compound is normally regarded as being made up of two parts, a positively charged or cationic part and a negatively charged or anionic part. To be stable the resulting compound must be electrically neutral with the anionic and cationic charges balancing. The cationic part is normally composed of metallic elements, while the anionic part can be formed of either a non-metallic ion such as oxygen or a combination of several elements forming an anionic group, such as a carbonate (CO_3), sulphate (SO_4), or silicate (SiO_4, etc.).

The forces binding together the various atoms in a mineral are essentially electrical in nature. Known as bonds, they play a large part in determining a mineral's chemical and physical properties. The most important bonds are: 1) the metallic bond, common in the native metals and some sulphides; 2) the covalent bond, of most importance in organic compounds but also found in some minerals, e.g. diamond (Fig. 1); 3) the ionic bond, the most important in mineralogy as over 90% of the known mineral species can be considered as ionic compounds.

In the Earth's crust eight elements (oxygen, silicon, aluminium, iron, calcium, sodium, potassium, magnesium) form the bulk of the rock-forming silicate minerals and constitute nearly 99% of its mass.

Table I Chemical elements commonly found in minerals, arranged in order of increasing atomic weight

element	symbol	element	symbol	element	symbol
hydrogen	H	calcium	Ca	cadmium	Cd
lithium	Li	titanium	Ti	tin	Sn
beryllium	Be	vanadium	V	antimony	Sb
boron	B	chromium	Cr	barium	Ba
carbon	C	manganese	Mn	lanthanum	La
nitrogen	N	iron	Fe	cerium	Ce
oxygen	O	cobalt	Co	tantalum	Ta
fluorine	F	nickel	Ni	tungsten	W
sodium	Na	copper	Cu	platinum	Pt
magnesium	Mg	zinc	Zn	gold	Au
aluminium	Al	arsenic	As	mercury	Hg
silicon	Si	strontium	Sr	lead	Pb
phosphorus	P	yttrium	Y	bismuth	Bi
sulphur	S	zirconium	Zr	thorium	Th
chlorine	Cl	molybdenum	Mo	uranium	U
potassium	K	silver	Ag		

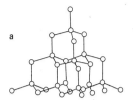
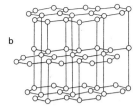

Fig. 1 *The structure of diamond (a) and graphite (b). Both minerals are covalent compounds and composed of pure carbon. Diamond crystallizes in the cubic system but graphite is hexagonal and the planes of structural weakness in graphite can be clearly seen. This results in graphite being one of the softest minerals whereas diamond is the hardest.*

Crystals

Mineralogy is a science largely concerned with the crystalline state. A crystal is a body bounded by smooth plane surfaces (faces) that are the external expression of an orderly internal atomic arrangement. Minerals, when occurring under conditions favourable to crystal growth, will form well developed crystals. However, if the growing crystals interfere with each other they are often poorly formed or distorted. The mineral is still described as crystalline, for no matter how imperfectly formed, it has the same ordered atomic structure and definite chemical composition. Even before the development of the advanced scientific techniques we know today, it was realized that the arrangement of the faces on a crystallized mineral and the angles between these faces were characteristic for that given mineral species. This means that, no matter how poorly formed the crystal is, or of what habit, the angle between the same two faces (if developed) in all crystals of the same mineral species is constant (Fig. 2). This regularity of faces and angles led to the understanding that crystals were symmetrical bodies and could be classified according to that symmetry.

Fig. 2 *The law of constancy of interfacial angles. Crystals of the same mineral may assume different shapes due to the unequal development of the faces, yet the angles between similar faces remain constant.*

Symmetry

Ideas related to symmetry are therefore important in describing the shapes of crystals and their internal atomic arrangement. To subdivide crystals into symmetry groups three elements of symmetry are used. 1) *Planes of symmetry* Crystals can be symmetrical about a plane; that is, if a crystal is cut in half along that plane, one half will be the mirror image of the other. 2) *Axis of symmetry* Crystals can be symmetrical about an imaginary line or axis passing through their centre. For instance, a cube has a four-fold symmetry axis passing at right angles through the centre of any of its faces (Fig. 3). If rotated it appears the same four times in each complete rotation. A rectangular block has only a two-fold axis of symmetry passing at right angles through the centre of any face, and on rotation the same faces occur only twice in a revolution. 3) *Centre of symmetry* Crystals sometimes have a centre of symmetry when a face on the crystal has a corresponding parallel face on the other side of the crystal. On the basis of these symmetry elements, crystallographers assign crystals to six crystal classes. A seventh class (trigonal) is recognized by most mineralogists (Table II). This has the same set of reference axes as the hexagonal system but has a vertical three-fold axis of symmetry.

Table II Crystal axes and symmetry in the seven crystal classes

System	Axes	Symmetry
Cubic	Three equal axes mutually perpendicular	Four three-fold axes
Tetragonal	Three axes at right-angles, two of equal length	One four-fold axis
Hexagonal	Three equal axes in a horizontal plane and a fourth of different length perpendicular to this plane	One six-fold axis
Trigonal	As for hexagonal	One three-fold axis
Monoclinic	Three axes of unequal length, two of which are not at right-angles	One two-fold axis
Triclinic	Three unequal axes, none at right-angles	A centre of symmetry *or* no symmetry

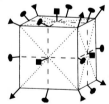

Fig. 3 *Planes of symmetry (shown as dotted and broken lines) and axes of symmetry in a cube.* ● *represents a two-fold axis,* ▲ *a three-fold axis, and* ■ *a four-fold axis.*

Crystal form

All the crystal faces of a mineral having a similar appearance and a like position with respect to the elements of symmetry for that particular mineral are said to have the same form. A crystal form therefore consists of all those faces required by the symmetry of the crystal. Crystals of the same mineral often show a range of different shapes according to which crystal forms or combinations of forms are developed (Fig. 4). Some forms such as the cube and octahedron totally enclose space and can form crystals by themselves; these are called *closed forms* (Fig. 5). Some forms, however, are termed *open forms*, that is, they do not enclose a volume of space and so can only form solid crystals if they occur in combination with other forms. Prisms, for instance, are an open form and in prismatic crystals the ends are terminated by other faces (forms), e.g. pyramids. The cubic system having the highest symmetry has fifteen forms in all, some of which are rarely observed. The common forms are the tetrahedron (4-faced), the cube (6-faced), the octahedron (8-faced), the dodecahedron (12-faced) and the icositetrahedron (24-faced). Many combinations of these can occur.

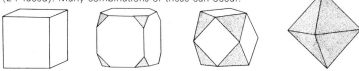

Fig. 4 *Combinations of the cubic and octahedral forms.*

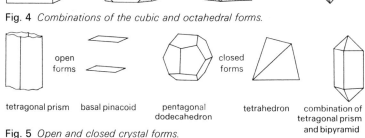

open forms

basal pinacoid

closed forms

tetragonal prism   basal pinacoid   pentagonal dodecahedron   tetrahedron   combination of tetragonal prism and bipyramid

Fig. 5 *Open and closed crystal forms.*

Crystal habit

Another important aspect in the study of crystals is the overall shape of the crystal known as its habit. This feature can be so characteristic of a particular mineral that often no other is needed to establish its identity (Fig. 6). Most minerals occur as aggregates of crystals, large single crystals being comparatively rare. Descriptive terms are applied to the form of the aggregates:

Botryoidal	resembling a bunch of grapes
Reniform	kidney-shaped
Globular	more or less spherical
Fibrous	consisting of long thin crystals
Foliated or lamellar	consisting of sheets that easily split apart
Radiating	spreading outward from a single point
Dendritic	resembling a fern.

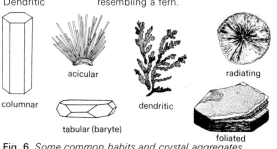
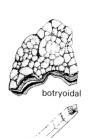

columnar   acicular   dendritic   radiating   botryoidal   tabular (baryte)   foliated   bladed

Fig. 6 *Some common habits and crystal aggregates.*

9

Twinning

Twinned crystals are those having the appearance of two or more individual crystals (in contact or interpenetration), that are identical and mirror images of one another. The individual parts of the twin must be related by a definite crystallographic law. Such crystals are usually described as either simple or repeated, contact or penetration twins. They may be interpenetrant as in staurolite; or repeatedly twinned (polysynthetic), if the successive twinned composition surfaces are parallel, as in plagioclase feldspars; or cyclic, if the composition surfaces are not parallel, often forming geniculate twins as in rutile.

Optical properties

Colour

The colour shown by a mineral is due to the selective absorption of certain wavelengths of white light by the mineral. The resulting colour is virtually white light minus the absorbed wavelengths. The causes of the colour in minerals are varied and complex and identification of specimens by this alone needs care since single species can show a wide range of colour. Sometimes colour is directly related to chemical composition, as in the typical blues and greens of most secondary copper minerals. However, it may be due to differences in the crystal structure or bonding (graphite and diamond) or to crystal growth defects, or also sometimes to contained impurities and inclusions.

Transparency

A very obvious property of a mineral specimen is its tendency to be either transparent, translucent or opaque. This property is a measure of the amount of light absorbed by the mineral, this being dependent upon the internal structure and chemical bonding of the mineral.

Lustre

The nature of a mineral's surface is the controlling factor in the amount of light reflected. Different surfaces produce different intensities of lustre and various terms are applied to describe these grades of lustre. *Metallic lustre*. This is shown by those minerals which are similar to metals; they absorb light strongly and are therefore opaque even in the thinnest fragments. *Non-metallic lustre*. There are various types of non-metallic lustre:

Vitreous	having a lustre characteristic of broken glass
Resinous	similar to that of resin
Adamantine	similar to that of diamond
Pearly	a lustre resulting from the reflection of light from parallel surfaces within the crystal
Silky	the lustre produced by the presence of fine parallel fibres as in some varieties of gypsum
Earthy	lack of lustre due to surfaces that scatter the light.

Minerals that have little or no lustre at all are described as dull.

Streak

The colour of the fine powder of a mineral is known as its streak. When a specimen is drawn across a piece of unglazed porcelain, known as a streak plate, a line of colour (streak) may result. This test is frequently used in mineral identification especially in the field because, although the colour of a mineral may vary greatly, the colour of the streak is usually constant.

Physical properties

Specific gravity (S.G.)

This is defined as the ratio of the weight of a given volume of mineral to the weight of an equal volume of water. It is a property which is dependent largely on the chemical nature of the atoms in the mineral and on the atomic packing in the structure. Instances occur of minerals of the same chemical composition having different S.G.'s due to denser atomic packing. Also minerals with a similar structure may have different S.G.'s due to the presence of heavier atoms in the structure. Minerals often show a range of S.G.'s due to chemical substitution. For example, the S.G. of the tetrahedrite series varies between 4·6 and 5·1 as a result of the replacement of arsenic by antimony in the structure.

Hardness

This is the ability of a metal to resist scratching or abrasion by other minerals or materials. It is related to the internal atomic structure and to the strength of the chemical bonding of the mineral. Mineralogists use the scale of hardness devised by F. Mohs in which ten minerals are arranged in an order of increasing hardness so that each will scratch those lower in the scale.

1 Talc (softest) 2 Gypsum 3 Calcite 4 Fluorite 5 Apatite 6 Orthoclase 7 Quartz 8 Topaz 9 Corundum 10 Diamond (hardest)

An unknown mineral is tested by deciding whether or not minerals of the Mohs' scale scratch the specimen. A hand lens is often necessary to be positive of the result. For field tests it is useful to know that the fingernail has a hardness of about $2\frac{1}{2}$; a steel pocket-knife blade about $5\frac{1}{2}$; and minerals of 6 and over will scratch glass. Quantitative hardnesses of materials are determined from the size of an indentation produced in the material by a controlled load, but these can still be related to the Mohs' scale.

Cleavage

Many minerals show cleavage, that is, the property of crystals to break readily in certain directions along plane surfaces. Cleavage surfaces are always parallel to crystal faces or possible crystal faces. This property is dependent upon the atomic structure, and in this case, the bond strength between different atoms, or planes of atoms, in the structure. For instance, in the mica group of minerals, chemical bonds between the silicon-oxygen layers are weak and the micas therefore cleave or split easily into thin sheets. The degree of perfection of cleavage varies between minerals so that less than *perfect* cleavages are described as *good, poor,* or *indistinct*. Where the mineral species has the property of cleavage, it usually shows in all specimens of that mineral, but parting is a property which may appear in some specimens of a mineral but not in all. Parting planes arise where stress develops planes of structural weakness along which crystals may be broken, for instance, twin crystals often part along the twin composition plane. Occasionally when a mineral specimen is broken it does not cleave or part along any definite plane, but simply fractures to leave an irregular surface. The nature of this irregular surface may be characteristic of the mineral and is known as the *fracture.* Different fractures are described as:

Conchoidal	typical of quartz, flint and sometimes glass, usually smooth curved surfaces like the interior of a shell (Fig. 7).
Splintery	breaks into splinters
Hackly	breaks with a jagged, irregular surface with sharp edges
Uneven or irregular	rough surfaces.

 Fig. 7 *Conchoidal fracture, the commonest type of fracture surface found in minerals.*

Tenacity
This is a property closely linked with the hardness of a mineral but defined as its toughness. A mineral is classed as *sectile* when it can be cut with the blade of a knife without powdering. If the specimen powders or breaks easily, it is decribed as *brittle.* The term *malleable* is used if a section of the specimen can be hammered flat without powdering and is typical of the native metals. If thin fragments of the material can be bent without breaking, and remain bent, they are known as *flexible,* whereas *ductile* means that the material can be drawn into a wire.

Other properties

Magnetism. Minerals that are attracted to a magnet are said to be magnetic. The minerals magnetite and pyrrhotine are the most common of the magnetic minerals. Other minerals showing varied magnetic properties are described in the minerals classification section.

Fluorescence. Some minerals become luminescent during exposure to ultra-violet light. The colour of the luminescence is usually characteristic of the species present. However, not all specimens of the same species show fluorescence as this may be due to fluorescence caused by impurities in the specimen.

Radioactivity. A number of species containing radioactive elements emit radioactivity. This can be tested with a Geiger counter. Most specimens of primary and secondary uranium and thorium minerals will exhibit this property.

There are many varied chemical tests which can be applied to fragments of mineral specimens to help in identification, usually by determining the elements present in the mineral, but you should have access to good laboratory facilities before performing these tests. However, the reaction of dilute or concentrated acids on certain minerals is characteristic; for example, the action of hydrochloric acid on carbonates producing effervescence, is typical. Also certain minerals when volatilized in a flame, will give a characteristic colour to a flame if certain elements are present; e.g. barium colours a flame apple-green. The test is best performed using the powdered mineral on a piece of platinum wire.

Rocks and mineral deposits

All rocks are composed of mineral grains and the major minerals present in a rock serve as a basis of petrological classification. In many coarse-grained rocks, such as granites, individual mineral grains can be clearly seen with the naked eye, whereas in basalts and other fine-grained rocks, microscopic examination is required.

Igneous rocks

Igneous rocks are formed by the solidification of molten rock material known as *magma*. Most magma is thought to originate within the Earth from a layer of dense rock called the *mantle* lying beneath the less dense *crust*. The crust is about 35 km thick under the continents but as little as 7 km under the oceans. Magma rising through the crust towards the Earth's surface crystallizes as *igneous intrusions*, such rocks usually being of a medium- to coarse-grain size. Magma reaching the surface is extruded as *lava* which cools rapidly resulting in a fine-grained appearance. The most common rock formed as a lava is the dark and dense rock known as *basalt*, whereas the most common intrusive rock is *granite*. The classification of igneous rocks is based on an assessment of the grain size and mineralogical composition – the important minerals used in this classification are quartz, the feldspars, feldspathoids, pyroxenes, amphiboles, micas, and olivines.

Metamorphic rocks

Metamorphism is the process by which pre-existing sedimentary and igneous rocks are mineralogically and texturally altered by heat and pressure within the Earth. As these processes take place generally at temperatures below the melting point of the rock, metamorphic minerals grow in a solid environment. Typical of these minerals are garnet, staurolite and kyanite. *Contact metamorphic rocks* are produced by high temperatures but low pressures, and are to be found near the contact with an igneous intrusion (metamorphic aureole – Fig. 8). Metamorphism on a larger scale, involving mountain building and other tectonic activities, results in *regionally metamorphosed rocks*. Their formation takes place at high temperatures and high pressures, kyanite and sillimanite being typical minerals formed under these conditions. Rocks formed under high pressure usually show a marked foliated texture, as in the common metamorphic rocks known as *schists* and *gneisses*. *Slates* have a similar appearance but can in addition be split into sheets. *Hornfels* is a fine-grained, even-textured rock resulting from thermal metamorphism. Most changes in metamorphic rocks take place in the solid state, but often movement of fluids through a rock occurs and this may give rise to chemical reactions, or it may add or remove material from the rock. This process is known as *metasomatism* and it occurs particularly around contact metamorphic deposits.

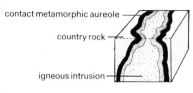

Fig. 8 *The contact metamorphic aureole surrounding an igneous intrusion.*

Sedimentary rocks
This important group of rocks is formed by surface processes on the Earth and the minerals involved are therefore products of low temperatures and pressures.

Sediments originating *mechanically* are composed of solid particles of weathered or abraded rock transported by water, wind or ice, forming sedimentary deposits in lakes, river mouths or seas. The particles subsequently become compacted into rocks of which typical types are conglomerates (coarse-grained), sandstones (medium-grained) or shales (fine-grained).

A *chemical* mode of origin applies to those sediments which precipitate or crystallize from solutions. *Evaporites* are a very important group under this heading forming when water evaporates from an enclosed body of sea-water or when the solution becomes saturated with salts. Rock salts, flints, and some limestones owe their origins to these and related processes.

Sediments formed *organically* result from the accumulation of organic material, such as bones or plant material and their subsequent consolidation into rocks. Oolitic limestone, chalk and coal are formed in this way.

Ore deposits
Of great importance to the demands of technology and the world economy are the metalliferous and non-metalliferous mineral deposits.

A number of heavy and relatively insoluble minerals such as gold, cassiterite and ilmenite readily form 'placer' or alluvial deposits after erosion and transportation from their original sites.

During the cooling and consolidation of some magmas, concentrations of certain minerals may form segregation deposits due to the gravity settling of the component crystals. The chromite-rich layers of the Bushveld complex in South Africa are an example.

As magma cools and crystallizes the remaining solution becomes more acidic and enriched with metallic components and other volatile and gaseous elements. These fluids may react with the pre-existing country rocks to form *contact metasomatic deposits*. For instance, residual liquids rich in boron and other volatiles lead to the extensive tourmalinization of many shales, slates or granites. During the final stages of magma consolidation highly

14

siliceous molten liquids may penetrate into the intrusive rocks and country rocks to form *pegmatite* veins. Comparatively rare minerals may form in large crystals in these veins: lithium minerals, phosphates, beryl and the niobates and tantalates are typical pegmatitic species.

The economically important sulphide ores are mainly deposited in the later stages of magma consolidation at temperatures between 50°C and 500°C. in what are known as *hydrothermal deposits*. These result from the crystallization of residual solutions in fractures and fissures in the surrounding rocks. These solutions form veins or lodes with both the ore and gangue minerals (minerals with no commercial value associated with the ore), often showing characteristic banding parallel to the wall of the vein. Often these fissures are not completely filled and 'cavities' or 'vugs' are formed, often being lined with well-developed crystals (Fig. 9). These vugs are eagerly sought after by mineral collectors for their mineral content.

Fig. 9 *A hydrothermal vein and a mineral-bearing vug.*

Replacement deposits are found when mineralizing solutions, instead of filling fractures, dissolve material and replace the rock. This is liable to occur in soluble rocks like limestones.

Fig. 10 *Weathering and secondary enrichment of a hydrothermal sulphide vein.*

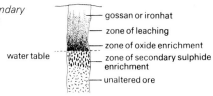

- gossan or ironhat
- zone of leaching
- zone of oxide enrichment
- zone of secondary sulphide enrichment
- unaltered ore

water table

Secondary enrichment involves the alteration of hydrothermal deposits by weathering processes (Fig. 10). Water descending through a hydrothermal vein from the Earth's surface takes the ore minerals into solution leaving a cavernous leached rock rich in silica and iron oxides ('gossan' or 'ironhat'). The metals become concentrated in the oxidizing solutions and will be deposited as a concentrated layer of oxide minerals. Below the water table an area of oxygen deficiency occurs and metals remaining in solution are redeposited as secondary sulphides rather than sulphates and carbonates. Below this level the vein reverts to its original unaltered state. The zone of secondary enrichment therefore often contains the redeposited metals from several hundred metres of leached rock.

The minerals described in this book are arranged in a conventional chemical sequence. The descriptions are made under four main headings habit, colour, occurrence and distinguishing properties; the last being those properties of the mineral species which are most important in identification.

Native elements

Gold

Au Cubic **Habit** Crystals are rare (cubic, octahedral and dodecahedral); usually dendritic growths, occasionally as rounded masses. Often as alluvial grains. Twinning is common on octahedral planes. **Colour** Golden-yellow, lighter yellow with increasing silver content; opaque. Golden-yellow streak. Metallic lustre. **Occurrence** Small amounts in hydrothermal veins, associated commonly with quartz and pyrite. Due to resistance to chemical alteration and density, the grains become concentrated into alluvial deposits, and may be consolidated into conglomerates. **Distinguishing properties** Colour; S.G. 19·3 pure; hardness $2\frac{1}{2}$–3; insoluble in single acids; hackly fracture; malleable and ductile. Pyrite (fool's gold) and chalcopyrite are readily distinguished from gold by their greater hardness and brittle nature.

Silver

Ag Cubic **Habit** Crystals are rare, sometimes cubic, octahedral or dodecahedral, usually massive, scaly or wiry aggregates. Twinning is common on octahedral planes. **Colour** Silver-white tarnishing rapidly to grey or black; opaque. Metallic lustre. Silver-white streak. **Occurrence** Usually in hydrothermal veins, or in the oxidized zone of silver-bearing ore deposits. Sometimes found in conglomerates or placer deposits. **Distinguishing properties** Colour, black tarnish; S.G. 10·5 (for the pure metal), silver often contains considerable gold or mercury (mercury-rich varieties are known as amalgam); hardness $2\frac{1}{2}$–3; hackly fracture; malleable and ductile. Soluble in nitric acid.

Copper

Cu Cubic **Habit** Crystals usually cubic or dodecahedral, commonly occurring as dendritic forms, or wire-like crystal growths. Twinning is common on octahedral planes. **Colour** Bright copper-red on fresh surfaces tarnishing to a dull brown colour and often superficially coated with black or green crusts; opaque. Metallic-copper red streak. Metallic lustre. **Occurrence** Commonly found in the oxidized zones of copper deposits associated with cuprite, malachite and azurite. Also often associated with basic extrusive igneous rocks where copper has formed by the reaction of copper-bearing solutions with iron minerals. **Distinguishing properties** Habit; colour and tarnish; S.G. 8·9; hardness $2\frac{1}{2}$–3; hackly fracture; malleable and ductile. Soluble in nitric acid.

Platinum

Pt Cubic **Habit** Found as rare cubic crystals, usually in grains, scales or nuggets. **Colour** Steel-grey to silver-white; opaque. Metallic lustre. White to steel-grey streak. **Occurrence** In basic and ultrabasic igneous rocks, associated with olivine, pyroxene, chromite and magnetite, where it may form rich magmatic segregations. Also found as grains or nuggets in river gravels derived from areas of ultrabasic rocks. **Distinguishing properties** Colour; S.G. 14–19 (21·5. for pure metal), native platinum always contains iron, often copper and other platinum-group metals; hardness 4–$4\frac{1}{2}$; hackly fracture; malleable. Insoluble in all acids apart from hot aqua regia.

Iron and Nickel-iron

Fe and Fe-Ni Cubic **Habit** Native iron occurs very rarely as a terrestrial mineral in the form of grains and sometimes larger masses. In meteorites nickel-iron occurs intergrown as kamacite (Fe,Ni with 4–7% Ni) with taenite (Fe,Ni with 30–60% Ni) lamellar masses. **Colour** Steel-grey to black; opaque. Metallic lustre. Iron-grey streak. **Occurrence** Terrestrial native iron occurs rarely where volcanic rocks cut coal seams. The most important occurrence is on Disko Island in west Greenland. **Distinguishing properties** Strongly magnetic; S.G. 7·3–8·2; hardness 4–5; poor cubic cleavage; hackly fracture; malleable.

Arsenic

As Hexagonal (Trigonal) **Habit** Crystals are very rare, usually massive, occurring as granular or botryoidal masses. **Colour** Light grey on fresh surfaces, rapidly tarnishing to dark grey; opaque. Metallic lustre. Light grey streak. **Occurrence** As a constituent of some hydrothermal veins commonly associated with silver, cobalt and nickel minerals. **Distinguishing properties** Habit; characteristic garlic odour when heated. Can easily be confused with native antimony but when heated on a charcoal block arsenic volatilizes whereas antimony melts to a metallic globule. S.G. 5·6–5·8; hardness $3\frac{1}{2}$; perfect basal cleavage; uneven granular fracture.

Antimony

Sb Hexagonal (Trigonal) **Habit** Crystals are rare, usually massive, occurring as lamellar, botryoidal or reniform (kidney-shaped) masses. Twinning is common. **Colour** Light grey; opaque. Metallic lustre. Grey streak. **Occurrence** In hydrothermal veins, associated with silver minerals, often associated with stibnite, also sphalerite, pyrite and galena. **Distinguishing properties** Habit; distinguished from arsenic by the lack of characteristic odour on heating. S.G. 6·6–6·7; hardness 3–3½; perfect basal cleavage; uneven fracture.

Bismuth

Bi Hexagonal (Trigonal) **Habit** Rare as crystals, usually granular masses or in reticulated or arborescent forms. Twinning is frequent, often polysynthetic. **Colour** Silver-white, with a reddish hue which darkens with exposure. Often an irridescent tarnish is developed; opaque. Metallic lustre. Silver-white, shiny streak. **Occurrence** In hydrothermal veins, associated with ores of cobalt, nickel, silver and tin. **Distinguishing properties** Distinguished from antimony by colour, melts readily at 270°C forming a product soluble in nitric acid. S.G. 9·7–9·8; hardness 2–2½; perfect basal cleavage; brittle when cold, malleable when heated.

Sulphur

S Orthorhombic **Habit** Crystals thick tabular or bipyramidal, also as massive, stalactitic or powdery aggregates. **Colour** Bright yellow to yellowish brown; transparent to translucent. Resinous to greasy lustre. White streak. **Occurrence** As a sublimation product of volcanic gases, encrusting volcanic vents or fumaroles; also deposited from some thermal springs. Sulphur is most commonly found in sedimentary rocks associated with gypsum and limestone; often occurs in the cap rocks of salt domes in association with anhydrite, gypsum and calcite. **Distinguishing properties** Colour; S.G. 2·0–2·1; hardness $1\frac{1}{2}$–$2\frac{1}{2}$; uneven to conchoidal fracture; slightly sectile. Low melting point (113°C); insoluble in water and dilute hydrochloric acid but soluble in carbon disulphide.

Diamond

C (pure carbon) Cubic **Habit** Commonly occurs as octahedral crystals also cubic, dodecahedral, tetrahedral, often with curved faces. Twinning is common on the octahedral plane. **Colour** Colourless, sometimes pale yellow, blue, green, red or even black; transparent to translucent. Gem quality diamonds are clear. The colour and transparency of diamonds vary greatly and have a considerable bearing on their value. Bort is a grey to black variety, due to impurities and inclusions. Adamantine to greasy lustre. White streak. **Occurrence** Sporadically distributed in ultrabasic rocks rich in olivine and phlogopite (kimberlites), which form pipe-like intrusions. Also in alluvial deposits, mainly as river and beach gravels. **Distinguishing properties** Habit and lustre; S.G. 3·5; extreme hardness 10; perfect octahedral cleavage; conchoidal fracture.

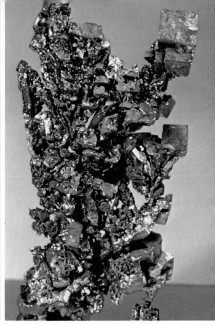

Graphite

C (pure carbon) Hexagonal **Habit** Flat tabular crystals, commonly massive, foliated, granular or earthy. **Colour** Black; opaque. Dull metallic or earthy lustre. Dark grey (pencil lead) streak, readily marks paper. **Occurrence** Formed by metamorphism of rocks having an appreciable carbon content. It can be found in crystalline limestones, schists, quartzites and metamorphosed coal-beds. Also found in some igneous rocks, veins and pegmatites. **Distinguishing properties** Colour; S.G. 2·1–2·3; hardness 1–2 (Extreme softness, greasy feel); perfect basal cleavage; sectile. Distinguished from molybdenite, a mineral of similar appearance, by its black streak, lower S.G. and colour.

Sulphides and sulphosalts

Argentite (Silver glance)

Ag_2S Cubic. Argentite is stable above 180°C, acanthite is the monoclinic modification which is stable below 180°C. **Habit** Crystals are commonly cubic or octahedral (paramorphs of acanthite after argentite). Frequently occurs as groups of crystals in parallel growth, also occurring as massive arborescent or filiform (wiry) aggregates. **Colour** Black; opaque. Metallic lustre. Black, shiny streak. **Occurrence** As a primary mineral in hydrothermal veins in association with pyrargyrite, proustite and native silver. Sometimes as microscopic inclusions in galena (argentiferous galena) **Distinguishing properties** Colour; S.G. 7·2–7·4; hardness 2–2½; poor cubic cleavage; subconchoidal fracture; sectile. Soluble in dilute nitric acid.

Chalcosine (Chalcocite, Copper Glance)

Cu_2S Orthorhombic **Habit** Crystals are short prismatic or thick tabular; usually massive. Twinning is common, giving pseudohexagonal forms. **Colour** Dark grey to black; opaque. Metallic lustre. Black streak. **Occurrence** Most commonly found in the secondary enriched zone of primary copper sulphides often associated with native copper or cuprite. Also in hydrothermal veins with chalcopyrite covelline and pyrite. **Distinguishing properties** Colour; association with other copper minerals. S.G. 5·5–5·8; hardness $2\frac{1}{2}$–3; prismatic indistinct cleavage; conchoidal fracture. Soluble in hot nitric acid. Often shows alteration to malachite or azurite.

Bornite (Peacock Ore, Erubescite)

Cu_5FeS_4 Cubic **Habit** Crystals are cubic or dodecahedral, the faces of which are often rough or curved; usually massive. Twinning is on the octahedral plane. **Colour** Copper-red to brown, tarnishing rapidly to a characteristic purplish iridescence; opaque. Metallic lustre. Pale grey to black streak. **Occurrence** A common copper mineral found in hydrothermal veins, both as a primary constituent and as a product of secondary enrichment. **Distinguishing properties** Colour and iridescent tarnish (Peacock Ore). S.G. 5.1; hardness 3; uneven to subconchoidal fracture. Alters to chalcosine, cuprite, malachite and azurite. Soluble in nitric acid.

Galena

PbS Cubic **Habit** Crystals are usually cubic, octahedral or cubo-octahedral, also massive or granular. Penetration and contact-twins on octahedral plane. **Colour** Lead-grey; opaque. Metallic lustre. Lead-grey streak. **Occurrence** Very widely distributed, the most important lead-ore. Found extensively in hydrothermal sulphide vein deposits associated with sphalerite, pyrite, chalcopyrite, tetrahedrite, bournonite and gangue minerals. In some high temperature veins and replacement deposits associated with garnet, diopside, rhodonite and biotite. Also as a replacement body in limestone and dolomite rocks. **Distinguishing properties** Colour and metallic lustre; S.G. 7·4–7·6; hardness $2\frac{1}{2}$; perfect cubic cleavage. Oxidizes readily to anglesite, cerussite, pyromorphite or mimetite.

Sphalerite (Blende)

ZnS Cubic **Habit** Crystals commonly tetrahedral or dodecahedral, often distorted with rough curved faces, also occurs massive, granular and sometimes fibrous. Twinning is common on octahedral plane. **Colour** Commonly yellow, brown to black with increasing iron content, sometimes red; transparent to translucent. Resinous to sub-metallic lustre. Brown to light yellow streak. **Occurrence** The most common zinc mineral. Occurs in hydrothermal ore veins, associated with other sulphides; as replacement orebodies in limestone, associated with pyrite, pyrrhotine and magnetite. **Distinguishing properties** Colour and lustre; S.G. 3·9–4·1; hardness $3\frac{1}{2}$–4; perfect dodecahedral cleavage; conchoidal fracture. Slowly soluble in hydrochloric acid with evolution of hydrogen sulphide. May alter to hemimorphite or smithsonite.

Chalcopyrite (Copper Pyrites)

$CuFeS_2$ Tetragonal **Habit** Crystals often of tetrahedral appearance; usually massive. Contact, interpenetration, or lamellar twins. **Colour** Brass-yellow, sometimes with iridescent tarnish; opaque. Metallic lustre. Greenish-black streak. **Occurrence** Very common copper mineral widespread in medium- to high-temperature hydrothermal veins. Chalcopyrite is the primary copper mineral of most 'porphyry-copper' deposits. Also found in pegmatites, schists and some contact metamorphic rocks. **Distinguishing properties** Colour and tarnish; S.G. $4 \cdot 1$–$4 \cdot 3$; hardness $3\frac{1}{2}$–$4\frac{1}{2}$; poor cleavage; uneven fracture; brittle. Soluble in nitric acid. Distinguished from pyrite by lower hardness; gold by brittle character and pyrrhotine by colour and lack of magnetism.

Wurtzite

ZnS Hexagonal **Habit** Found as pyramidal crystals, also occurs radiating, fibrous massive. **Colour** Brownish black; opaque to translucent. Resinous lustre. Brown streak. **Occurrence** Rather rare; an unstable high temperature modification of sphalerite (stable above 1020°C) with which it often occurs intergrown; usually found in sulphide ores formed from acidic fluids. **Distinguishing properties** Habit; S.G. $4 \cdot 0$–$4 \cdot 1$; hardness $3\frac{1}{2}$–4; distinct prismatic cleavage; even to conchoidal fracture.

Greenockite

CdS Hexagonal **Habit** Occurs rarely as pyramidal crystals, usually as a powdery coating. **Colour** Orange-yellow; translucent. Adamantine to resinous lustre. Orange-yellow to brick-red streak. **Occurrence** Most important cadmium mineral. Found as a yellow coating to zinc minerals such as sphalerite. Small crystals are found at several localities associated with prehnite and natrolite in cavities in basalts. **Distinguishing properties** Colour; habit; S.G. 4·9; hardness $3-3\frac{1}{2}$; distinct prismatic, imperfect basal cleavage; conchoidal fracture. Soluble in hydrochloric acid giving off hydrogen sulphide gas.

Pyrrhotine (Pyrrhotite, Magnetic Pyrites)

FeS Hexagonal. Usually shows a deficiency of iron, the formula varying from FeS to $Fe_{0.8}S$. Troilite which has a composition close to the ideal FeS is found only in meteorites. **Habit** Mostly massive, granular, but occasionally as rosettes of hexagonal platy crystals. **Colour** Bronze-yellow, tarnishing to brown; opaque. Metallic lustre. Greyish black streak. **Occurrence** Occurs principally in basic igneous rocks such as gabbro, and as disseminated grains. Also found in pegmatites, in contact metamorphic deposits or high-temperature sulphide veins and replacement bodies. **Distinguishing properties** Colour; magnetic; S.G. 4·6–4·7; hardness $3\frac{1}{2}-4\frac{1}{2}$; basal parting; subconchoidal to uneven fracture. Distinguished from chalcopyrite by colour and magnetism and from pyrite by colour and hardness.

Nickeline (Niccolite)

NiAs Hexagonal **Habit** Occurs rarely as pyramidal crystals, usually massive in reniform or columnar aggregates. **Colour** Pale copper-red often alters on surfaces to pale green annabergite (nickel bloom). Metallic lustre. Pale brownish-black streak **Occurrence** Found with pyrrhotine, chalcopyrite and other nickel sulphides in basic igneous rocks; also in hydrothermal vein deposits with cobalt and silver minerals. **Distinguishing properties** Colour and alteration; S.G. 7·8; hardness 5–5½; lack of cleavage; uneven fracture. Soluble in nitric acid giving a green solution.

Millerite

NiS Hexagonal (Trigonal) **Habit** Usually as acicular needles, often in radiating groups. **Colour** Brass-yellow; opaque. Metallic lustre. Greenish black streak. **Occurrence** Frequently as tufts of slender crystals in cavities in limestone or dolomite, often as an alteration product of other nickel-rich minerals. As a late stage mineral in hydrothermal deposits. **Distinguishing properties** The fibrous yellow crystals of millerite with their characteristic metallic lustre are readily identifiable. S.G. 5·3–5·6; hardness 3–3½; perfect rhombohedral cleavage; uneven fracture.

Pentlandite

$(Fe,Ni)_9S_8$ Cubic **Habit** Massive, usually as granular aggregates. **Colour** Bronze-yellow; opaque. Bronze-brown streak. Metallic lustre. **Occurrence** The mineral is one of the most important ores of nickel. Usually found in basic igneous rocks with iron and nickel sulphides and arsenides, accumulated by magmatic segregation. Usually found intergrown with pyrrhotine. **Distinguishing properties** Not easily distinguished from pyrrhotine except in polished section. S.G. 4·6–5.0; hardness $3\frac{1}{2}$–4; lack of cleavage; conchoidal fracture.

Covelline (Covellite)

CuS Hexagonal **Habit** Crystals are rare, usually in hexagonal plates; mostly massive. **Colour** Indigo blue, often iridescent to brass-yellow or purplish-red; opaque except in very thin fragments. Metallic lustre. Dark grey to black streak. **Occurrence** Usually found in the zone of secondary enrichment with chalcosine, bornite and chalcopyrite formed by the alteration of primary sulphides. Also sometimes found in hydrothermal veins as a primary sulphide. **Distinguishing properties** Colour and perfect basal cleavage distinguish covellite from chalcosine and bornite. S.G. 4·6–4.8; hardness $1\frac{1}{2}$–2.

Cinnabar

HgS Hexagonal (Trigonal) **Habit** Crystals are usually rhombohedral or thick tabular, sometimes short prismatic; also granular, massive. Twinning is common with basal pinacoid as twin plane. **Colour** Scarlet-red to brownish red; transparent to translucent, occasionally opaque. Adamantine to submetallic lustre in opaque specimens. Vermilion streak. **Occurrence** Cinnabar is the most important mercury mineral. Usually found in veins or impregnations formed at low temperatures near recent volcanic rocks or hot springs. Associated with pyrite, stibnite and realgar. **Distinguishing properties** Colour; S.G. 8·0–8·2; hardness 2–2$\frac{1}{2}$; prismatic perfect cleavage; subconchoidal fracture; slightly sectile. In the zone of weathering cinnabar may alter to native mercury or mercurous chloride (calomel).

Realgar

AsS Monoclinic **Habit** Short prismatic crystals, striated parallel to their length; also occurs as granular or massive aggregates. **Colour** Bright red-orange to orange-yellow; transparent to translucent. Resinous to greasy lustre. Red-orange streak **Occurrence** In low temperature hydrothermal deposits associated with orpiment, stibnite and other arsenic minerals. Also in deposits from hot springs and as a volcanic sublimate. **Distinguishing properties** Colour; S.G. 3.5; hardness 1$\frac{1}{2}$–2; Good pinacoidal cleavage; conchoidal fracture; sectile. Often associated with orpiment. Specimens should be kept in darkened containers as the mineral disintegrates on exposure to light forming a yellowish powdery mixture of orpiment and arsenolite (As_2O_3).

Orpiment

As_2S_3 Monoclinic **Habit** Rarely occurs as short prismatic crystals, usually as foliated or granular masses associated with realgar. **Colour** Lemon-yellow to brownish-yellow; transparent to translucent. Resinous to pearly lustre. Pale yellow streak. **Occurrence** As a low temperature mineral formed in hydrothermal veins and certain hot spring deposits, often associated with realgar from which it forms as an alteration product. **Distinguishing properties** Colour and association with realgar; S.G. 3·5; hardness $1\frac{1}{2}$–2; one perfect cleavage; pearly lustre on cleavage surfaces.

Stibnite (Antimony Glance)

Sb_2S_3 Orthorhombic **Habit** Stout or slender elongated, prismatic crystals, striated parallel to their length, crystals are sometimes bent or twisted. Commonly found in aggregates of acicular crystals or as radiating or columnar masses, sometimes granular. **Colour** Lead-grey, sometimes with blackish to iridescent tarnish; opaque. Metallic lustre. Lead-grey streak. **Occurrence** The most common antimony mineral. Commonly found in low-temperature hydrothermal veins with quartz, also as replacement bodies in limestone and in certain hot spring deposits. Often associated with orpiment, realgar, galena, pyrite and cinnabar. **Distinguishing properties** Habit; S.G. 4·5–4·6; hardness 2; one perfect cleavage parallel to length of crystals; subconchoidal fracture. Melts readily, even in a match flame. Soluble in hydrochloric acid.

Bismuthinite (Bismuth Glance)

Bi_2S_3 Orthorhombic. Isostructural with stibnite **Habit** Prismatic to acicular crystals; usually massive, foliated or fibrous. **Colour** Lead-grey to tin-white, sometimes with an iridescent tarnish; opaque. Metallic lustre. Lead-grey streak. **Occurrence** Found in high-temperature hydrothermal veins associated with native bismuth, arseno-pyrite, quartz and other sulphides. **Distinguishing properties** Habit; S.G. 6·8; hardness 2; one perfect cleavage. Less flexible but more sectile than stibnite. Dissolves in nitric acid with a white precipitate on dilution.

Pyrite (Iron Pyrites)

FeS_2 Cubic **Habit** Crystals commonly cubic, also as pyritohedra. Cubic faces are often striated with the striations perpendicular to those on adjacent faces. Also found massive or as nodules. Fossils are often replaced by pyrite. Frequently twinned to form interpenetrant crystals. **Colour** Pale brass-yellow; opaque. Metallic lustre. Greenish or brownish black streak. **Occurrence** Pyrite is one of the most widely distributed sulphide minerals. It is present in igneous rocks as an accessory mineral or as segregations; common in hydrothermal veins, in replacement and contact metamorphic deposits. It occurs in black shales formed under anaerobic conditions. **Distinguishing properties** Colour; lack of tarnish; S.G. 4·9–5·2; hardness 6–6½; poor cubic cleavage; conchoidal to uneven fracture. From chalcopyrite by hardness. Soluble in nitric acid, insoluble in hydrochloric acid.

Marcasite

FeS_2 Orthorhombic . **Habit** Crystals are commonly tabular; also massive, stalactitic or as radiating fibres. Twinning is common often repeated, producing 'spear-shaped' or 'cockscomb' like crystal groups. **Colour** Pale bronze-yellow; opaque. Metallic lustre. Greyish or brownish black streak. **Occurrence** Marcasite occurs most often in near surface deposits, deposited at lower temperatures than pyrite. Also in low-temperature hydrothermal veins with zinc and lead ores. Frequently found in sedimentary rocks limestones, especially chalk or clays often as concretions or replacing fossils. **Distinguishing properties** Colour; habit; distinctive spear-shaped twins; S.G. 4.8–4.9; hardness $6-6\frac{1}{2}$; distinct prismatic cleavage; uneven fracture. Decomposes more readily than pyrite.

Cobaltite

$CoAsS$ Cubic **Habit** Sometimes as cubes or pyritohedra or combinations of these forms, faces often striated as in pyrite; commonly massive. **Colour** Silver-white to steel-grey often with a reddish tinge; opaque. Metallic lustre. Grey-black streak. **Occurrence** In high-temperature hydrothermal veins associated with arsenopyrite, skutterudite and nickeline, also as disseminated grains in metamorphic rocks. **Distinguishing properties** Colour; S.G. 6·3; hardness $5\frac{1}{2}$; perfect cubic cleavage; uneven fracture. Sometimes alters to pink erythrite (cobalt bloom).

Arsenopyrite (Mispickel)

FeAsS Monoclinic **Habit** As short prismatic crystals, faces often striated. Columnar crystals have a rhombic cross-section; granular or massive. Twinning is common on prism, as contact, penetration or as cruciform twins; forms pseudo-orthorhombic crystals. **Colour** Silver grey-white, often with a brownish tarnish; opaque. Metallic lustre. Greyish-black streak. **Occurrence** The most abundant arsenic mineral. Forms under moderately-high temperature conditions, occurring with gold-quartz veins and also ores of tin, tungsten and silver, with pyrite, chalcopyrite, sphalerite and galena. Also found in limestones, dolomites, gneisses and pegmatites. **Distinguishing properties** Colour; S.G. 5·9–6·2 (some cobalt often substitutes for iron); hardness $5\frac{1}{2}$–6; indistinct prismatic cleavage; uneven fracture.

Molybdenite

MoS_2 Hexagonal **Habit** Crystals are hexagonal, often tabular; commonly foliated or scaly masses, also granular, massive. **Colour** Lead-grey sometimes with bluish tinges, opaque. Metallic lustre. Greenish-grey streak, bluish-grey on paper. **Occurrence** The most common molybdenum mineral. Found as an accessory mineral in some granites or pegmatites and in hydrothermal veins with scheelite, wolframite, topaz and fluorite. Also in contact metamorphic deposits with garnet, pyroxene, scheelite and pyrite. **Distinguishing properties** Can only be confused with graphite but its colour, lustre and density are characteristic. S.G. 4·6–4·7; hardness 1–$1\frac{1}{2}$; perfect basal cleavage; flexible laminae; sectile.

Skutterudite, Smaltite (illustrated) and Chloanthite Series

The three minerals form an isomorphous series with the general formula. (Co,Ni) As_{2-3} Cubic **Habit** Crystals occur as cubes, octahedra or cubo-octahedra usually massive or granular. **Colour** Tin-white to silver-grey, iridescent or greyish tarnish; opaque. Metallic lustre. Black streak. **Occurrence** Found in medium-temperature hydrothermal veins, with cobaltite, nickeline, arsenopyrite, silver and bismuth. **Distinguishing properties** Habit; S.G. $6.1-6.9$; hardness $5\frac{1}{2}-6$; distinct cubic and octahedral cleavages; conchoidal to uneven fracture. High cobalt members yield erythrite on weathering, rarer high nickel members, green annabergite. Chemical tests are required to distinguish the group from arsenopyrite.

Pyrargyrite

Ag_3SbS_3 Hexagonal (Trigonal) **Habit** Usually in hexagonal prisms with pyramidal terminations; also massive, compact. Twinning is common, forming 'swallow-tail' crystal groups. **Colour** Deep red, darkens on exposure to light; translucent to nearly opaque, transparent in thin fragments. Adamantine lustre. Dark red streak. **Occurrence** Pyrargyrite and proustite are commonly called ruby silver ores. Found in low-temperature silver veins, one of the last primary minerals to crystallize. Associated with native silver, argentite, tetrahedrite, galena and sphalerite. **Distinguishing properties** Can be confused with proustite but pyrargyrite has a deeper red colour. Its habit distinguishes it from cuprite. S.G. 5.8; hardness $2\frac{1}{2}$; distinct rhombohedral cleavage; conchoidal to uneven fracture.

Proustite

Ag_3AsS_3 Hexagonal (Trigonal) Isostructural with pyrargyrite. **Habit** Prismatic crystals, sometimes rhombohedral or scalenohedral; also massive, compact. Twinning is common. **Colour** Scarlet, darkens on exposure to light; transparent to translucent. Adamantine lustre. Bright red streak **Occurrence** Found together with pyrargyrite in silver veins, but is less common. **Distinguishing properties** Colour and streak; S.G. 5·6; hardness $2-2\frac{1}{2}$; distinct rhombohedral cleavage; conchoidal to uneven fracture. After heating proustite forms a malleable globule of silver whereas pyrargyrite gives a brittle globule.

Tetrahedrite (illustrated) – Tennantite

$(Cu_{12}Sb_4S_{13})$-$(Cu_{12}As_4S_{13})$ Cubic. These are the end members of a continuous solid-solution series in which arsenic substitutes for antimony. Iron also substitutes for some copper, and silver is often present. **Habit** Crystals are commonly tetrahedral; also massive, granular compact. Contact or penetration twins on tetrahedron. **Colour** Dark grey to black; opaque. Metallic lustre. Brown to black streak. **Occurrence** Tetrahedrite is commonly found in low-to medium-temperature hydrothermal veins associated with copper, lead, silver and zinc minerals, also found in contact metamorphic deposits. Tennantite is not as common. **Distinguishing properties** Habit and colour; S.G. 4·6–5·1 (tetrahedrite higher than tennantite); hardness $3-4\frac{1}{2}$; subconchoidal to uneven fracture. Oxidizes to malachite and azurite.

Enargite

Cu_3AsS_4 Orthorhombic   **Habit**
Crystals are commonly striated prisms,
or tabular. Often massive; granular,
bladed or columnar. Occasionally forms
star-shaped trillings (three individuals).
Colour Dark grey to black; opaque.
Metallic lustre. Black streak.   **Occurrence** The mineral is found in vein
and replacement deposits formed at
low to medium temperatures associated
with chalcosine, bornite, covelline,
pyrite, sphalerite, galena, baryte and
quartz. **Distinguishing properties** The
tabular striated crystals are very characteristic. S.G. 4·4; hardness 3; perfect
prismatic cleavage (present even in
granular specimens), pinacoidal distinct; uneven fracture. It fuses easily
and will melt in a match flame.

Bournonite

$PbCuSbS_3$ Orthorhombic   **Habit**
Crystals are usually short prismatic or
tabular; also occurs as massive or
granular. Twinning is very common,
repeated twinning produces cruciform
or cog-wheel-like crystal aggregates.
Colour Steel-grey to black; opaque.
Metallic lustre (usually bright on the
edges of cog-wheel twins, but dull on
the broad flat faces). Grey to black
streak. **Occurrence** Found in medium-
temperature hydrothermal veins, associated with galena, tetrahedrite,
sphalerite, chalcopyrite, pyrite and
rarely stibnite. Highly prized specimens
came from the Herodsfoot mine,
Liskeard, Cornwall.   **Distinguishing
properties** Habit of twinned crystals;
S.G. 5·7–5·9; hardness $2\frac{1}{2}$–3; poor
prismatic cleavage; subconchoidal to
uneven fracture.

Boulangerite

$Pb_5Sb_4S_{11}$ Monoclinic **Habit** Elongated prismatic to acicular crystals; usually striated along the direction of elongation; often in fibrous masses. **Colour** Bluish lead-grey; opaque. Metallic lustre. Brownish grey streak. **Occurrence** In low-to medium-temperature hydrothermal veins, often associated with galena, stibnite, sphalerite, pyrite and other lead-antimony minerals; also with quartz, calcite and dolomite. **Distinguishing properties** Habit; S.G. 6·0–6·2; hardness $2\frac{1}{2}$–3; one good cleavage; generally brittle but thin fibres are flexible. Similar in physical properties to stibnite and jamesonite but it has a higher specific gravity than both of these minerals. X-ray study often required for positive identification.

Jamesonite

$Pb_4FeSb_6S_{14}$ Monoclinic **Habit** Acicular to fibrous crystals, striated along the direction of elongation; often in felted masses; also massive, columnar. **Colour** Grey black, sometimes with iridescent tarnish; opaque. Metallic lustre. Grey-black streak. **Occurrence** In medium-temperature hydrothermal veins, associated with other sulphides and sulpho-salts. **Distinguishing properties** Habit; S.G. 5·6 (lower than boulangerite); hardness 2–3; good basal cleavage. Dissolves in hot hydrochloric acid giving the characteristic 'rotten egg' odour of hydrogen sulphide. Crystals are not flexible like those of stibnite.

Oxides

Cuprite

Cu_2O Cubic **Habit** Crystals are usually small modified octahedra, sometimes cubes or dodecahedra, also as fine acicular crystals (var. chalcotrichite); often massive, granular. **Colour** Dark red, sometimes nearly black (var. chalcotrichite — red fibres); translucent, sub-transparent when thin fragments. Adamantine to submetallic lustre. Brownish red streak. **Occurrence** Often found as a secondary mineral in the oxidized zone of copper sulphide deposits. **Distinguishing properties** Habit and colour; associated minerals; S.G. 6·1; hardness $3\frac{1}{2}$–4 (softer than hematite and harder than cinnabar); poor octahedral cleavage; conchoidal to uneven fracture. Cuprite is soluble in hydrochloric acid staining the solution blue on dilution.

Zincite

ZnO Hexagonal **Habit** Crystals very rare (hexagonal pyramids); usually massive, foliated or granular. **Colour** Orange-yellow to deep red; translucent. Subadamantine lustre. Orange-yellow streak. **Occurrence** Zincite is a rare mineral except for a few localities such as Franklin, New Jersey, U.S.A. where it occurs in association with calcite, franklinite and willemite. **Distinguishing properties** Characteristic association; red colour and streak; S.G. 5·7; hardness 4; perfect prismatic cleavage; conchoidal fracture. Dissolves in hydrochloric acid.

Franklinite

(Zn,Mn,Fe)(Fe,Mn)$_2$O$_4$ Cubic. A member of the spinel group (see page 48). **Habit** Crystals octahedral, also massive, granular. **Colour** Black; opaque. Metallic lustre. Reddish-brown to dark brown streak. **Occurrence** Franklinite, zincite and willemite occur together in the zinc deposits of Franklin, New Jersey. The deposits are associated with crystalline limestone and are probably of a metasomatic origin. **Distinguishing properties** S.G. 5·0–5·2; hardness $5\frac{1}{2}$–$6\frac{1}{2}$; lack of cleavage; uneven fracture. Slightly magnetic.

Corundum (Ruby, Sapphire)

Al$_2$O$_3$ Hexagonal (Trigonal) **Habit** Crystals are commonly tabular; also rough, steep pyramidal 'spindle-shaped' prismatic forms; also massive, granular. Emery is a mixture of granular corundum, magnetite and spinel. Twinning is common, and often lamellar producing striations. **Colour** Blue (sapphire), pink to red (ruby) also yellow, brown, green, single crystals sometimes show colour variations; transparent to translucent. Adamantine to vitreous lustre. White streak. **Occurrence** Most abundant in marble schists and gneisses. In some pegmatites and certain nepheline syenites. Also in alluvial gravels as 'placer' deposits. **Distinguishing properties** Habit; S.G. 3·9–4·1; hardness 9 (great hardness); lack of cleavage; basal parting; uneven to conchoidal fracture.

Hematite

Fe_2O_3 Hexagonal (Trigonal) **Habit**
Crystals are often thin tabular, sometimes as rosettes (iron rose); also
rhombohedral with curved, striated
faces. Commonly massive. Compact
aggregates, often in characteristic
mamillated or botryoidal forms (kidney
ore). Penetration twins on basal pinacoid. **Colour** Steel-grey to black.
Massive compact varieties – dull to
bright red; opaque. Metallic lustre. Red
to reddish brown streak. **Occurrence**
Hematite is the most important ore of
iron and is widely distributed. Chiefly
found in thick beds of sedimentary
origin. In metamorphosed sediments
and contact metamorphic deposits.
Distinguishing properties Colour and
streak; S.G. 4·9–5·3; hardness 5–6;
lack of cleavage; uneven fracture.
Soluble in concentrated hydrochloric
acid.

Ilmenite

$FeTiO_3$ Hexagonal (Trigonal) **Habit**
Crystals are commonly thick tabular;
often massive, compact. Twinning is
common on basal pinacoid. **Colour**
Iron-black; opaque. Metallic to submetallic lustre. Black streak. **Occurrence** Common accessory mineral in
igneous rocks such as gabbros, diorites
and anorthosites. Also found in ore
veins and pegmatites, and as alluvial
or beach sands. The mineral is an
important source of the metal titanium.
Distinguishing properties S.G. 4·8;
hardness 5–6; parting on basal plane;
conchoidal fracture; distinguished from
hematite by its black streak and from
magnetite by its lack of magnetism.

Braunite

$3Mn_2O_3.MnSiO_3$ Tetragonal **Habit** Found mostly as pyramidal crystals; also massive, granular crystals sometimes appear to be pseudo-octahedral. **Colour** Brownish-black to steel-grey; opaque. Submetallic lustre. Brownish-black to steel-grey streak. **Occurrence** Often found in hydrothermal veins with other manganese oxides, also formed as the product of metamorphism of manganese bearing sediments. **Distinguishing properties** Colour and crystal form. S.G. 4·7–4·8; hardness 6–6½; perfect pyramidal cleavage; uneven fracture. Soluble in hydrochloric acid, leaving a residue of silica.

Rutile

TiO_2 Tetragonal **Habit** Crystals commonly prismatic, faces often striated, sometimes acicular, rarely pyramidal; also massive, granular. Twinning is common on bipyramid, forming knee-shaped twins, or complex cyclic twins made up of 6 or 8 individuals. **Colour** Usually reddish-brown to red, sometimes black (iron-, tantalum-, and niobium-bearing); transparent to translucent, black specimens opaque. Adamantine to metallic lustre. Pale brown streak. **Occurrence** Widespread accessory mineral in igneous rocks, also in quartzites, schists and gneisses. Also concentrated in alluvial deposits and beach sands. Often occurs as acicular crystalline inclusions in quartz. **Distinguishing properties** Colour; habit and twinning; S.G. 4·2–5·6 (niobium and tantalum varieties); hardness 6–6½; distinct prismatic cleavage; uneven fracture.

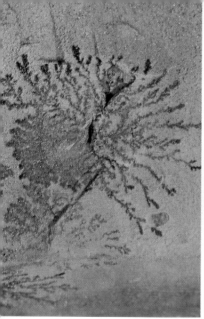

Pyrolusite

MnO_2 Tetragonal **Habit** Crystals are rare, sometimes found in form of elongated prisms. Usually occurs in reniform sooty masses which soil the hands when touched. Also very common as dendritic encrustations (see illustration above) in narrow fissures. **Colour** Dark grey; opaque. Metallic to dull lustre. Black streak. **Occurrence** Pyrolusite is a secondary mineral formed by the oxidation of manganite and other primary manganese minerals. Often found associated with hausmannite, braunite, goethite and limonite. **Distinguishing properties** Habit. Dissolves in conc. hydrochloric acid giving off chlorine gas. Only distinguishable from psilomelane if crystals are visible. S.G. 5·06 for crystals, lower when massive; hardness $6–6\frac{1}{2}$ for crystals, massive 2–6; perfect prismatic cleavage; uneven fracture.

Cassiterite (Tinstone)

SnO_2 Tetragonal **Habit** Crystals are usually short prismatic or pyramidal; also massive, granular. Also as fibrous botryoidal crusts or masses (wood tin) or waterworn pebbles' (stream tin). Twinning is common forming contact and penetration twins, often repeated. **Colour** Usually reddish brown to nearly black; nearly transparent to opaque. Adamantine and splendant lustre. White or light grey to brown streak. **Occurrence** A high temperature mineral occurring in hydrothermal veins and pegmatites closely associated with granitic rocks. Commonly associated with wolframite, arsenopyrite, topaz, quartz and tourmaline. Abundant in some alluvial deposits. **Distinguishing properties** Habit and colour; lustre and streak; S.G. 7·0; hardness 6–7; imperfect prismatic cleavage; subconchoidal to uneven fracture.

Anatase (Octahedrite)

TiO_2 Tetragonal **Habit** Crystals commonly bipyramidal; also tabular. **Colour** Various shades of yellow and brown, deep blue or black; transparent to nearly opaque. Adamantine lustre. White to pale yellow streak. **Occurrence** As an accessory mineral in igneous and metamorphic rocks. Formed at relatively low temperatures and frequently found in veins or fissures in schists and gneisses. Commonly associated with quartz, brookite and rutile. Occasionally in granite pegmatites. Also as a detrital mineral. **Distinguishing properties** Habit and colour; S.G. 3·8–4·0; hardness $5\frac{1}{2}$–6; perfect basal and pyramidal cleavages; subconchoidal fracture.

Brookite

TiO_2 Orthorhombic **Habit** Crystals are usually thin tabular, platy or prismatic. **Colour** Reddish-brown to brownish-black; translucent. Metallic to adamantine lustre. White to yellow streak. **Occurrence** As an accessory mineral in igneous and metamorphic rocks and in hydrothermal veins where it forms at relatively low temperatures. Often found as detrital grains. **Distinguishing properties** Habit and colour; S.G. 4·1; hardness $5\frac{1}{2}$–6; poor prismatic cleavage; subconchoidal to uneven fracture. Rutile, anatase and brookite are polymorphs of TiO_2.

Tungstite (Tungsten Ochre)

$WO_3 \cdot H_2O$ Orthorhombic   **Habit**
Occasionally found as microscopic
platy crystals; generally massive, earthy.
Colour   Yellow to yellowish green;
translucent. Resinous lustre. Yellow
streak. **Occurrence** Usually formed
by the oxidation of wolframite and is
usually found associated with it in
tungsten deposits. **Distinguishing
properties** Colour and association with
wolframite. S.G. 5·5; hardness $2\frac{1}{2}$;
perfect basal cleavage.

Uraninite (Pitchblende)

UO_2 Cubic **Habit** Crystals are rare,
cubic with octahedral modifications.
Usually occurs as massive, botryoidal
(pitchblende) or earthy. **Colour**
Brownish-black   or   greyish-black;
opaque. Submetallic to greasy or
pitch-like lustre; dull. Brownish-black
or greyish streak. **Occurrence** Crystallized uraninite occurs in some granite
and syenite pegmatites, associated
with zircon, tourmaline, monazite, mica
and feldspar. Pitchblende is usually
found as colloform crusts in high-
to medium-temperature hydrothermal
veins with cassiterite, pyrite, chalcopyrite, arsenopyrite and galena. Also
as a detrital mineral in some sedimentary quartz conglomerates. **Distinguishing properties** Habit; lustre;
S.G. 8–10 (crystals), 6·6–8·5 (massive);
hardness 5–6; conchoidal to uneven
fracture. Bright yellow or green alteration patches. Highly radioactive.

Brucite

Mg(OH)$_2$ Hexagonal (Trigonal) **Habit** Crystals usually broad tabular; commonly foliated massive, fibrous or fine granular. **Colour** White to pale grey, pale green or blue; transparent to translucent. Pearly lustre on cleavage surfaces, waxy to vitreous elsewhere. White streak. **Occurrence** In metamorphosed dolomitic limestones and also as a low-temperature hydrothermal mineral, often found in veins in serpentine. Usually associated with calcite, aragonite, talc and magnetite. **Distinguishing properties** Foliated habit and lustre; S.G. 2·4; hardness 2$\frac{1}{2}$; perfect basal cleavage; separable, flexible plates; sectile. Easily soluble in hydrochloric acid. Distinguished from talc by greater hardness and from gypsum by habit.

Lepidocrocite

FeO(OH) Orthorhombic **Habit** As tabular or scaly crystals; usually as micaceous, fibrous or massive aggregates. **Colour** Red to brown; transparent. Submetallic lustre. Dull orange streak. **Occurrence** Found as a secondary mineral, usually associated with goethite. **Distinguishing properties** Colour and streak; S.G. 3.9–4.1; hardness 5; perfect cleavage; brittle fracture.

Manganite

MnO(OH) Monoclinic (pseudo-orthorhombic) **Habit** Crystals prismatic, often striated and with blunt or flat terminations. Frequently grouped in bundles, also columnar to coarse fibrous. Contact or penetration twins on prism. **Colour** Black to dark grey; opaque. Submetallic lustre. Reddish brown to black streak. **Occurrence** In low-temerature hydrothermal veins, associated with granite rocks. Deposited in bogs, lakes, and shallow marine environments. Often found associated with pyrolusite, geothite and baryte. **Distinguishing properties** Habit; colour and streak; S.G. 4·3; hardness 4; perfect pinacoidal cleavage; uneven fracture. Soluble in concentrated hydrochloric acid, liberating chlorine gas. Infusible.

Bauxite

Bauxite is the name given to deposits rich in hydrous aluminium oxides. It is mostly a mixture of gibbsite, boehmite and diaspore. Bauxite occurs as massive, oolitic, pisolitic or earthy concretionary masses. Formed by prolonged tropical weathering and leaching of silica from rocks containing aluminium silicates.

Gibbsite (Hydrargillite) (illustrated)

$Al(OH)_3$ Monoclinic **Habit** Tabular crystals, usually massive as botryoidal, stalactitic encrustations, also foliated and earthy aggregates. Twinning is common. **Colour** White, grey, sometimes pink or red; transparent to translucent. Vitreous lustre, pearly on cleavages. White streak **Occurrence** in earthy or pisolitic bauxite. Also as a low-temperature hydrothermal mineral in aluminous igneous rocks. **Distinguishing properties** S.G. 2·4; hardness $2\frac{1}{2}$–$3\frac{1}{2}$; perfect basal cleavage.

Boehmite

AlO(OH) Orthorhombic **Habit** Microscopic tabular crystals; commonly disseminated or pisolitic aggregates. **Colour** White, dull, earthy lustre. White streak. **Occurrence** An important constituent of bauxite, formed by the weathering of aluminium silicate rocks low in quartz. **Distinguishing properties** Needs microscopic identification. S.G. 3·0–3·1; hardness 3; one good cleavage.

Diaspore (illustrated)

AlO(OH) Orthorhombic **Habit** .Crystals commonly thin platy, prismatic; also massive, foliated and scaly aggregates. **Colour** White to colourless, sometimes green, pink or brown; transparent to translucent. Vitreous lustre, pearly on cleavages. White streak. **Occurrence** Massive material occurs in bauxite deposits. With corundum in emery deposits, or as a hydrothermal alteration product of other aluminous minerals. **Distinguishing properties** Habit; S.G. 3·3–3·5; hardness $6\frac{1}{2}$–7; one perfect cleavage; conchoidal fracture.

Wad is a mixture of several hydrous manganese oxides, such as pyrolusite (p. 41) and psilomelane (p. 47). Similar in appearance to both these minerals and found in deposits formed in lakes and bogs under highly oxidizing conditions.

Psilomelane

Monoclinic. Psilomelane is one of a number of hydrous manganese oxides often occurring as a mixture of fine-grained or earthy botryoidal masses. The name is now applied to the mineral in which barium is an important constituent (cryptomelane with potassium, and coronadite where lead predominates) **Colour** Black to dark grey; opaque. Submetallic to dull lustre. Brownish black streak. **Occurrence** A secondary mineral precipitated at atmospheric temperatures together with pyrolusite, goethite, and limonite. Often forms as residual deposit resulting from the weathering of manganese carbonates or silicates. Concretionary forms common in lake and swamp deposits. **Distinguishing properties** Botryoidal, concretionary appearance; streak; S.G. 4·4–4·7; hardness 5–7 (lower for earthy material).

Goethite (illustrated)

FeO(OH) Orthorhombic **Habit** Crystals are platy, bladed or prismatic, usually massive, stalactitic, botryoidal or radiating fibrous; sometimes earthy. **Colour** Dark brown to yellowish-brown; opaque. Adamantine to dull lustre. Often silky due to fibrous structure. Brownish-yellow streak **Occurrence** As a secondary mineral, found in the oxidation zone of veins containing iron minerals. Also formed as a direct precipitate in bogs or lagoons. **Distinguishing properties** Colour; habit; S.G. 3·3–4·3; hardness 5–5½; one perfect cleavage; uneven fracture. Sometimes magnetic after strong heating.

Limonite is an impure hydrated iron oxide, largely composed of goethite. Brown coloured, with a yellow-brown streak. Found mainly as botryoidal or weathered crusts, formed by the oxidation of iron minerals or as a precipitate in bog or marine deposits.

47

Spinel

$MgAl_2O_4$ Cubic A series of minerals of similar structure, which includes $MgAl_2O_4$ (spinel) $FeAl_2O_4$ (hercynite) $ZnAl_2O_4$ (gahnite) $MnAl_2O_4$ (galaxite). **Habit** Crystals are usually octahedral; also massive. Twinning is common on octahedron (spinel twins). **Colour** Variable; commonly red (ruby spinel) but also blue, green, brown, black to colourless; transparent (magnesium-rich) to opaque. Vitreous lustre. White streak (spinel); grey (gahnite); green (hercynite); red-brown (galaxite). **Occurrence** As an accessory mineral in igneous rocks. In metamorphosed aluminous schists and in contact metamorphosed limestones in which gem quality spinels occur; also in alluvial deposits derived from these. **Distinguishing properties** Habit and twinning; S.G. 3·5–4·1; hardness $7\frac{1}{2}$–8; octahedral parting; conchoidal to uneven fracture. Infusible.

Magnetite

Fe_3O_5 Cubic. A member of the spinel group. **Habit** Commonly as octahedral crystals, also dodecahedral, often massive, granular. Twinning is common on octahedron (spinel twins). **Colour** Black; opaque. Metallic to submetallic lustre. Black streak. **Occurrence** As an abundant and widely distributed oxide mineral. Commonly found as an accessory mineral in igneous rocks, and as magmatic segregation deposits with pyroxene and apatite. It is a common mineral in contact and regionally metamorphosed calcareous rocks with garnet, diopside, pyrite and chalcopyrite, also in some high-temperature mineral veins. Also as a detrital mineral in beach or river sands. **Distinguishing properties** Habit and colour; streak; S.G. 5·2; hardness $5\frac{1}{2}$–$6\frac{1}{2}$; octahedral parting; subconchoidal to uneven fracture. Strongly magnetic.

Chromite

$FeCr_2O_4$ Cubic. A member of the spinel group, often contains some magnesium (magnesio-chromite) or aluminium. **Habit** Crystals are rare but octahedral; usually massive, granular. **Colour** Black; opaque. Metallic lustre. Brown streak. **Occurrence** As an accessory mineral in igneous rocks such as peridotite and serpentinite, in these it is often concentrated into layers or lenses. Also found in alluvial sands or gravels. Chromite is the sole source of chromium metal which is widely used in the production of stainless steels. **Distinguishing properties** Brown streak and weak magnetism distinguishes chromite from magnetite. S.G. 4.1–5.1; hardness $5\frac{1}{2}$; uneven fracture. Infusible.

Chrysoberyl (Alexandrite)

$BeAl_2O_4$ Orthorhombic **Habit** Crystals are usually tabular or short prismatic; also granular massive. Contact or penetration twins are common, often repeated forming pseudo-hexagonal crystals. **Colour** Green, yellow sometimes brownish; transparent to translucent. The transparent gem variety alexandrite is green in natural light but red by artificial light. A further gem variety, usually yellow-green, contains many fine, fibrous inclusions causing chatoyancy, 'cat's-eye', in polished samples. Vitreous lustre. White streak. **Occurrence** In granite pegmatites, also in mica schists. Frequently found in alluvial deposits. **Distinguishing properties** Habit and twinning; colour; S.G. 3·7–3·8; hardness $8\frac{1}{2}$; distinct prismatic cleavage; conchoidal to uneven fracture.

Pyrochlore (illustrated) and Microlite

$(Ca,Na)_2(Nb,Ta)_2O_6)O,OH,F)$ Cubic. Substitution for sodium and calcium occurs including uranium, thorium and rare earth elements. **Habit** Crystals commonly octahedral, also in irregular masses and as embedded grains. **Colour** Pyrochlore — various shades of brown to black; microlite — pale yellow to brown, sometimes shades of red or green; subtranslucent to opaque. Vitreous to resinous lustre. Streak is paler than its colour. **Occurrence** Usually found in pegmatites associated with alkaline igneous rocks, with zircon and apatite, tantalite and columbite. Pyrochlore is also found in igneous intrusions of carbonatite. Microlite is usually associated with granite pegmatites. **Distinguishing properties** Crystal form; colour; S.G. 4·2 (pyrochlore) to 5·5 (microlite); hardness 5–5½; distinct octahedral cleavage; subconchoidal to splintery fracture. Some specimens are radioactive due to uranium and thorium.

Columbite (illustrated) — Tantalite Series

$(Fe,Mn)(Nb,Ta)_2O_6$
$(Mn,Fe)(Ta,Nb)_2O_6$. Orthorhombic **Habit** Occurs as short or equant prismatic crystals, sometimes thin or thick tabular, may also form large groups of subparallel crystals; also massive. Twinning is common, usually as simple contact twins; also as repeated twins. **Colour** Iron-black to brownish black; reddish brown in thin splinters. Often an iridescent surface tarnish; subtranslucent to opaque. Submetallic to resinous lustre. Dark red to black streak. **Occurrence** Usually as a primary mineral in granite pegmatites. Also found in some detrital 'placer' deposits. **Distinguishing properties** Colour; crystal form; S.G. 5·2 (columbite) to 8.0 (tantalite); hardness 6 (columbite) to 6½ (tantalite); distinct pinacoidal cleavage; subconchoidal to uneven fracture.

Halides

Halite (Rock Salt)

NaCl Cubic **Habit** Cubic crystals often with hollow faces (hopper crystals); also massive and granular. **Colour** Colourless or white, also shades of yellow, red and blue (due to the presence of impurities); transparent to translucent. Vitreous lustre. White streak. **Occurrence** Halite is widely distributed in stratified beds formed by the evaporation of saline waters in enclosed basins. Thick deposits of halite associated with sylvine, gypsum and anhydrite occur in sedimentary basins. Also occurs as a volcanic sublimate. **Distinguishing properties** Habit and transparency; S.G. 2·1–2.2; hardness $2\frac{1}{2}$; perfect cubic cleavage; conchoidal fracture; salty taste; soluble in water.

Sylvine

KCl Cubic **Habit** Usually as cubic crystals sometimes octahedral; also massive, compact. **Colour** Colourless or white, also shades of grey, blue, yellow or red; transparent to translucent. Vitreous lustre. White streak. **Occurrence** Found in bedded salt-deposits such as those at Stassfurt, Germany and associated with, but less common than halite because of its greater solubility in water. Also found as encrustations in volcanic fumaroles especially at Mount Vesuvius. **Distinguishing properties** S.G. 2·0; hardness 2; perfect cubic cleavage; uneven fracture. Bitter taste.

Carnallite

$KMgCl_3.6H_2O$ Orthorhombic **Habit** Crystals are rare, sometimes pseudo-hexagonal or tabular; usually massive or granular. **Colour** Colourless to white, often red-orange due to minute hematite inclusions; transparent to translucent. Greasy, dull to shiny lustre. White streak. **Occurrence** In the upper-layers of evaporite deposits together with halite and sylvine. Together with sylvine the mineral is mined and used as a source of potassium for fertilizers. **Distinguishing properties** S.G. 1·6; hardness $2\frac{1}{2}$. Distinguished from other salts by the lack of cleavage; conchoidal fracture. Deliquescent; soluble in water. Bitter taste. Fuses readily when heated.

Fluorite (Fluorspar)

CaF_2 Cubic **Habit** Crystals usually cubic, sometimes octahedral or rhomb-dodecahedral; also massive, coarse to fine granular or compact. Interpenetrant twins common. **Colour** Colourless when pure, commonly purple, blue, green, yellow or brown, rarely pink or red. Blue-john is a massive, colour banded variety; transparent to translucent. Vitreous lustre. White streak. **Occurrence** Commonly in hydrothermal veins, particularly those associated with galena and sphalerite quartz and baryte. Also in some greisens, granites and high-temperature cassiterite veins. **Distinguishing properties** Habit; S.G. 3·2; hardness 4; perfect octahedral cleavages; sub-conchoidal to splintery fracture. Lack of effervescence with hydrochloric acid. Generally weakly fluorescent.

Cryolite

Na$_3$AlF$_6$ Monoclinic **Habit** Crystals are rare, sometimes pseudocubic in appearance; usually massive, coarsely granular. Twinning is very common, complex. **Colour** Colourless to white, also reddish and brownish; transparent to translucent. Vitreous to greasy lustre. White streak. **Occurrence** Found in major quantities at only a few localities. At Ivigtut in Greenland it occurs in a pegmatitic body associated with microcline, quartz, siderite, galena and fluorite. It was formally used as a flux in the electrolytic production of aluminium, but the synthetic compound is now generally used. **Distinguishing properties** Pseudocubic habit; lustre; S.G. 3·0; hardness 2$\frac{1}{2}$; basal and prismatic parting, to give cuboidal form. Fuses readily when heated.

Chlorargyrite (Horn Silver, Cerargyrite)

AgCl Cubic **Habit** Crystals cubic, but rare; commonly massive as waxy or horn-like masses. Twinning is on octahedral planes. **Colour** Colourless when fresh, usually grey becoming violet-brown on exposure to light; translucent. Resinous to adamantine lustre. White streak. **Occurrence** Secondary mineral occurring in the oxidized zones of silver deposits, especially in arid regions. Commonly associated with native silver, cerussite and limonite. **Distinguishing properties** Colour; S.G. 5·5–5·6; hardness 1$\frac{1}{2}$–2$\frac{1}{2}$; uneven to subconchoidal fracture; sectile and ductile. Melts readily when heated giving a silver globule.

Atacamite

$Cu_2(OH)_3Cl$ Orthorhombic **Habit** Commonly in slender, striated, prismatic crystals, sometimes tabular; also massive, fibrous or granular. Twinning occurs sometimes as doublets, trillings and other complex twins. **Colour** Bright green to dark green; transparent to translucent. Adamantine to vitreous lustre. Apple-green streak. **Occurrence** Found as a secondary mineral in the oxidized zone of copper deposits especially in arid, saline conditions. Often associated with malachite, cuprite, chrysocolla, brochantite, gypsum and limonite. **Distinguishing properties** Habit and colour; S.G. 3·8; hardness 3–3½; perfect pinacoidal cleavage; conchoidal fracture. Distinguished from malachite by lack of effervescence in hydrochloric acid.

Mendipite (illustrated with vein of chloroxiphite)

$Pb_3O_2Cl_2$ Orthorhombic **Habit** Crystals bladed or fibrous; sometimes massive. **Colour** Colourless to white or brownish grey; transparent to translucent. Pearly lustre on cleavages, resinous elsewhere. White streak. **Occurrence** Found in the manganese deposits of the Mendip Hills, Somerset, England. **Distinguishing properties** S.G. 7·2; hardness 2½; perfect prismatic cleavage and two other good cleavages; conchoidal to uneven fracture.

Chloroxiphite

$Pb_3CuCl_2O_2(OH)_2$ Monoclinic **Habit** Bladed crystals in subparallel groups. **Colour** Olive-green; translucent. Resinous to adamantine lustre. Pale yellow-green streak. **Occurrence** Rare secondary mineral associated with mendipite. **Distinguishing properties** S.G. 6·9–7·0; hardness 2½; one perfect and one distinct cleavage.

Carbonates

Calcite

$CaCO_3$ Hexagonal (Trigonal). Calcite is the stable form of $CaCO_3$ at most temperatures and pressures. Manganese and iron may substitute for calcium. **Habit** Crystals common and very varied. Four habits are common: tabular, prismatic, rhombohedral, and scalenohedral (dog tooth spar). Many combinations of these types may be found as well as fibrous, granular, stalactitic or massive aggregates. Twinning is common, usually the twin plane is either the basal pinacoid or a rhombohedral face. Lamellar twinning may also be produced by pressure. **Colour** Colourless (transparent) or white (opaque) when pure; often yellow or brownish (containing iron) pinkish (containing manganese or cobalt) also green, red, purple, blue, and black. Generally transparent to translucent. Vitreous lustre. White streak. **Occurrence** Very common, and found in many different environments. Often the major constituent of calcareous sedimentary rocks (lime-stone, chalk) and metamorphic rocks (marble). It may be precipitated directly from sea-water or as the material forming shells of living organisms which on death accumulate to form limestone. It is commonly found in veins associated with metallic ores. Sometimes replaces primary minerals in igneous rocks. Formed as a deposit of travertine or tufa from hot and cold calcareous springs. Stalactites and stalagmites are often formed of calcite. **Distinguishing properties** Habit; S.G. 2·7 (pure); hardness 3; perfect rhombo-hedral cleavage, despite the variable habit; conchoidal fracture. Effervesces freely in cold dilute hydrochloric acid. Infusible. Many specimens also fluoresce in ultraviolet light due to impurities.

Magnesite

$MgCO_3$ Hexagonal (Trigonal) **Habit** Crystals rare, but rhombohedral or prismatic; usually massive or granular, may be compact or fibrous. **Colour** White or colourless when pure, often grey, brown or yellowish when iron-bearing; transparent to translucent. Vitreous to earthy lustre. White streak. **Occurrence** Formed by the alteration of rocks consisting largely of magnesium silicates and by waters rich in carbonate. Found as stratiform beds of metamorphic origin with talc-chlorite or mica schists, also as a replacement of calcite rocks by magnesium bearing solutions. **Distinguishing properties** S.G. 3·0–3·2; hardness $3\frac{1}{2}$–$4\frac{1}{2}$; perfect rhombohedral cleavage; conchoidal fracture. Distinguished from dolomite and calcite by S.G. and lack of twinning. Will dissolve with effervescence in warm hydrochloric acid.

Siderite (Chalybite)

$FeCO_3$ Hexagonal (Trigonal) **Habit** Crystals commonly rhombohedral, frequently with curved or composite faces; also massive, granular, compact or fibrous. Twinning on rhombohedron, often lamellar. **Colour** Grey to yellowish brown; transparent to translucent. Vitreous lustre. White streak. **Occurrence** Widespread as bedded deposits in sedimentary rocks, these are often impure containing clays (clay-ironstone), carbonaceous material (blackband iron-ores) or calcium carbonate. Nodules of siderite are common in clay or shales. Also found as a gangue mineral in hydrothermal veins. **Distinguishing properties** Crystal form; from other rhombohedral carbonates by colour; S.G. 3·8–4·0; hardness $3\frac{1}{2}$–$4\frac{1}{2}$; perfect rhombohedral cleavage; uneven fracture. Soluble in hot hydrochloric acid with effervescence.

Rhodochrosite

$MnCO_3$ Hexagonal (Trigonal). Calcium and iron commonly substitute for manganese. **Habit** Crystals rhombohedral, rarely scalenohedral, usually with curved faces; mostly massive, compact or granular. **Colour** Pale to deep rose pink, yellowish grey, brownish; transparent to translucent. Vitreous lustre. White streak. **Occurrence** In low-temperature hydrothermal veins containing ores of silver, lead and copper. Sometimes found in high-temperature metasomatic deposits with garnet and rhodonite, and as a secondary mineral in residual or sedimentary manganese oxide deposits. **Distinguishing properties** From other rhombohedral carbonates by colour; S.G. 3·5–3·7; hardness $3\frac{1}{2}$–4; perfect rhombohedral cleavages; uneven fracture. Dissolves with effervescence in hot, dilute hydrochloric acid.

Smithsonite (Calamine)

$ZnCO_3$ Hexagonal (Trigonal). Iron and manganese may substitute for some zinc. **Habit** Crystals rare, but rhombohedral with rough, curved faces. Usually as botryoidal, reniform or stalactitic masses; also granular to compact, earthy or porous cavernous masses. **Colour** Shades of grey, brown or greyish-white also green, brown and yellow; translucent. Vitreous lustre. White streak. **Occurrence** Found in the oxidized zone of most zinc-ore deposits. It may also be found replacing calcareous rocks adjacent to the ore deposits. Usually associated with hemimorphite, cerussite, malachite, anglesite, and pyromorphite. **Distinguishing properties** Habit; S.G. 4·3–4·5 (high for a carbonate); hardness 4–$4\frac{1}{2}$; perfect rhombohedral cleavage (when observed); uneven fracture. Soluble in warm hydrochloric acid with effervescence. Infusible.

Dolomite

$CaMg(CO_3)_2$ Hexagonal (Trigonal). Iron often substitutes for magnesium. **Habit** Crystals commonly rhombohedral, with curved composite faces 'saddle-shaped'; also massive, coarse to fine granular, columnar and compact. Twinning is common, especially on basal plane and rhombohedron. **Colour** Colourless, usually white, often yellow, brown or pinkish; transparent to translucent. Vitreous to pearly lustre. White streak. **Occurrence** Common as a rock-forming mineral. Most 'sedimentary' dolomite results from the action of magnesium-rich solutions on pre-existing limestones. Occurs in hydrothermal veins with fluorite, baryte, siderite and calcite. Also as veins in serpentine, talcose rocks and altered basic igneous rocks. **Distinguishing properties** Habit; colour; S.G. 2·8–2·9; hardness $3\frac{1}{2}$–4; perfect rhombohedral cleavage; subconchoidal fracture. Reacts less readily with cold dilute hydrochloric acid (compare calcite) but effervesces readily when warm.

Ankerite

$Ca(Mg,Fe)(CO_3)_2$ Hexagonal (Trigonal). There is a series from dolomite to ankerite with iron substituting for magnesium. **Habit** Crystals are rhombohedral; also massive, granular. Twinning is common, similar to dolomite. **Colour** White, yellow, yellowish-brown sometimes grey, becomes dark brown on weathering or increasing iron content; translucent. Vitreous lustre. White streak. **Occurrence** Often found as a gangue mineral in sulphide veins especially associated with iron ores. Frequently fills joints in coal seams. **Distinguishing properties** Colour; S.G. 2·9–3·2; hardness $3\frac{1}{2}$–4; perfect rhombohedral cleavage.

Aragonite

CaCO₃ Orthorhombic **Habit** Crystals short to long prismatic, also acicular, often found in radiating groups; also reniform, globular or stalactitic. Untwinned crystal are rare; repeated twinning results in pseudo-hexagonal forms of both contact and penetration types. **Colour** Colourless, white, grey, yellowish, sometimes violet; transparent to translucent. Vitreous lustre. White streak. **Occurrence** Main component of the shells of many organisms (corals and oysters). As the primary precipitate of calcium carbonate from sea-water. As a deposit of hot springs often found with gypsum. Also in the oxidized zone of some ore deposits. **Distinguishing properties** S.G. 2·9; hardness $3\frac{1}{2}$–4; distinct pinacoidal cleavage; subconchoidal fracture. Dissolves with effervescence in cold dilute hydrochloric acid.

Witherite

BaCO₃ Orthorhombic **Habit** Crystals always twinned, often repeatedly twinned giving pseudo-hexagonal forms; also massive, granular, columnar or botryoidal. **Colour** Colourless, grey-white, pale yellow to brown; transparent to translucent. Vitreous lustre. White streak. **Occurrence** In some low-temperature hydrothermal veins associated with baryte and galena. **Distinguishing properties** Habit; S.G. 4·3; hardness 3–$3\frac{1}{2}$; distinct pinacoidal cleavage; uneven fracture. Soluble in dilute hydrochloric acid with effervescence. Powdered witherite will colour a flame apple-green (barium) readily distinguishing the mineral from strontianite (red).

Strontianite

$SrCO_3$ Orthorhombic **Habit** Prismatic crystals, often acicular and radiating; also massive, fibrous, columnar or granular. Contact twins common, often repeated to give pseudohexagonal forms. **Colour** Colourless, white, yellow, pale-green or brownish; transparent to translucent. Vitreous lustre. White streak. **Occurrence** Usually as a low-temperature hydrothermal mineral often associated with celestine, baryte and calcite. Also as concretionary masses in limestones or clay. **Distinguishing properties** Habit; S.G. 3·7; hardness $3\frac{1}{2}$–4; nearly perfect prismatic cleavage; uneven fracture. Soluble with effervescence in dilute hydrochloric acid. When powdered it colours a flame red (strontium).

Cerussite

$PbCO_3$ Orthorhombic **Habit** Crystals are common, often prismatic or tabular parallel to side, pinacoid, sometimes bipyramidal or pseudohexagonal forms; also massive, granular, compact and sometimes stalactitic. Twinning is very common, may be multiple, forming reticulated groups, star-shaped pseudohexagonal crystals or arrowhead twins. **Colour** Usually white or grey, sometimes darker colours due to impurities; transparent to translucent. Adamantine lustre. White streak. **Occurrence** A common secondary mineral found in the oxidized zone of ore deposits containing galena. **Distinguishing properties** Twinned forms; lustre; S.G. 6·4–6·6; hardness 3–$3\frac{1}{2}$; Distinct prismatic cleavage in two directions; conchoidal fracture. Dissolves with effervescence in warm dilute nitric acid.

Malachite

$Cu_2CO_3(OH)_2$ Monoclinic **Habit** Crystals rare, almost always found as botryoidal, stalactitic or encrusting masses. Often with a structure of compact radiating fibres, banded in various shades of green; also granular or earthy. Twinning is common. **Colour** Bright green, various shades; translucent. Fibrous varieties have silky lustre, rather dull when massive, crystals adamantine. Pale-green streak. **Occurrence** Common secondary copper mineral, often occurring in the oxidized zone of copper deposits. It may be found as pseudomorphs after azurite or cuprite. **Distinguishing properties** Habit; colour; S.G. 3·9–4·0 (some massive varieties as low as 3·6); hardness $3\frac{1}{2}$–4; perfect cleavage (rarely seen); subconchoidal to uneven fracture. Soluble with effervescence in dilute hydrochloric acid.

Azurite (Chessylite)

$Cu_3(CO_3)_2(OH)_2$ Monoclinic **Habit** Crystals often tabular or short prismatic, frequently complex in habit and malformed in development; also in radiating groups, massive or earthy. **Colour** Various shades of azure-blue; transparent to translucent. Vitreous to adamantine lustre. Pale-blue streak. **Occurrence** Found as a secondary copper mineral in the oxidized zone of copper deposits, often interbanded with malachite. Also associated with chrysocolla, chalcosine, calcite, limonite and other secondary copper minerals. **Distinguishing properties** Distinct crystals are common. Colour; S.G. 3·8; hardness $3\frac{1}{2}$–4; perfect prismatic cleavage, also pinacoidal; conchoidal fracture. Dissolves with effervescence in dilute hydrochloric acid. Frequently alters to malachite.

Leadhillite

$Pb_4(SO_4)(CO_3)_2(OH)_2$　Monoclinic
Habit　Crystals　often　pseudo-
hexagonal, thin to thick tabular occasionally prismatic or equant; also
massive, granular. Twinning is very
common, of several different types to
give pseudohexagonal, lamellar and
interpenetrant twins. **Colour** Colourless, white, grey, pale green, blue and
yellow; transparent to translucent.
Resinous to adamantine lustre. White
streak.　**Occurrence**　Found in the
oxidized zone of lead deposits as a
secondary mineral associated with
cerussite, anglesite, lanarkite, linarite,
pyromorphite and galena. **Distinguishing properties**　Habit and twinning;
S.G. 6·5–6·6; hardness $2\frac{1}{2}$–3; perfect
basal cleavage, splits into flexible
plates; conchoidal fracture. Dissolves
with effervescence in nitric acid leaving
a residue of lead sulphate. Breaks up in
hot water.

Aurichalcite

$(Zn,Cu)_5(OH)_6(CO_3)_2$ Orthorhombic
Habit As delicate acicular or slender
lath-like crystals. Commonly as tufted
aggregates　or　encrustations,　rarely
columnar, granular. **Colour** Pale green
to　greenish-blue,　sky-blue;　transparent. Silky to pearly lustre. Pale-
green or blue streak.　**Occurrence**
Widespread as a secondary mineral in
the　oxidized　zone　of　zinc-copper
deposits, rarely in pegmatites. **Distinguishing properties** Habit; colour;
S.G. 3·9–4·2; hardness 1–2; one perfect cleavage. Dissolves in hydrochloric and nitric acids.

Nitrates and Borates

Nitratine (Chile Saltpetre, Soda Nitre)

$NaNO_3$ Hexagonal (Trigonal) **Habit** Crystals are rare, rhombohedral; usually massive or granular, often as encrustations. Twinning is common. **Colour** Colourless or white, sometimes reddish-brown, grey or yellowish; transparent to translucent. Vitreous lustre. White streak. **Occurrence** Commonly found in arid regions as surface deposits, associated with gypsum, halite and other soluble nitrates and sulphates. **Distinguishing properties** Habit; S.G. 2·2–2·3; hardness 1–2; perfect rhombohedral cleavage; conchoidal fracture. Dissolves easily and completely in water. Deliquescent. Fuses easily giving bright-yellow emission (sodium).

Nitre

KNO_3 Orthorhombic **Habit** As thin encrustations or silky acicular crystals. Twinning is often multiple, forming pseudohexagonal twins. **Colour** White; translucent. Vitreous lustre. White streak. **Occurrence** Occurs with nitratine, as friable crusts on surface rocks. Also as a constituent of certain soils. The important deposits in Chile are exploited as a source of nitrates. **Distinguishing properties** Habit; S.G. 2·1; hardness 2; perfect cleavage. Dissolves easily in water but not deliquescent. Fuses easily with violet emission (potassium).

Borax

$Na_2B_4O_7.10H_2O$ Monoclinic **Habit** Crystals usually short prismatic; also massive. **Colour** Colourless or white, sometimes with tinges of blue, green or grey; translucent. Vitreous lustre. White streak. **Occurrence** Found in evaporite deposits, precipitated by the evaporation of salt lakes in arid regions. In association with other evaporite minerals such as halite, as well as sulphate and carbonate minerals and other borates. **Distinguishing properties** Habit; S.G. 1·7; hardness $2-2\frac{1}{2}$; perfect pinacoidal cleavage; conchoidal fracture. Easily fusible, with swelling. Colours a flame yellow (sodium). Soluble in water.

Colemanite

$Ca_2B_6O_{11}.5H_2O$ Monoclinic **Habit** Crystals are often highly modified but usually short prismatic; also massive, compact and granular. **Colour** Colourless white or grey; transparent to translucent. Vitreous to adamantine lustre. White streak. **Occurrence** As a lining to cavities or geodes in sedimentary rocks formed as a secondary mineral derived from waters passing through primary borate deposits, such as borax and ulexite. **Distinguishing properties** S.G. 2·4; hardness $4-4\frac{1}{2}$; one perfect cleavage; uneven fracture. Soluble in hot hydrochloric acid, with the separation of a white precipitate (boric acid) on cooling. Fuses easily.

Ulexite

$NaCaB_5O_9.8H_2O$ Triclinic **Habit** Usually in rounded masses of fine fibrous crystals (cotton balls) or as parallel fibrous aggregates; rare as elongate crystals. **Colour** Colourless (crystals) to white; transparent to translucent. Vitreous lustre (crystals), silky (aggregates). White streak. **Occurrence** An evaporite mineral occurring with borax in the surface deposits of arid areas. Also found in some bedded gypsum deposits. **Distinguishing properties** Habit; S.G. 1·9–2·0; hardness $2\frac{1}{2}$ (aggregated material has an apparent hardness of 1); perfect cleavage (crystals). Fuses easily in candle flame with swelling. Virtually insoluble in cold water, slightly soluble in hot. Tasteless.

Kernite

$Na_2B_4O_7.4H_2O$ Monoclinic **Habit** Usually found as coarse cleavable aggregates; crystals often stubby sometimes wedge-shaped, rounded and markedly striated. **Colour** Colourless, but usually chalky white due to surface alteration film of tincalconite $(Na_2B_4O_7.5H_2O)$; transparent. Vitreous to pearly lustre. White streak. **Occurrence** Found in a large deposit in the Mojave Desert of California, United States. Believed to have formed from an existing borax deposit by subsequent recrystallization caused by increased temperature and pressure. **Distinguishing properties** S.G. 1·9–2.0; hardness $2\frac{1}{2}$–3; two perfect cleavages, giving long splintery fragments. Slowly dissolves in cold water; readily dissolves in hot water.

Sulphates

Baryte (Barytes, Barite)

$BaSO_4$ Orthorhombic. Strontium substitutes for barium in solid solution series from baryte to celestine. **Habit** Crystals commonly tabular, often diamond shaped due to the development of vertical prisms, elongated prismatic crystals common; also as globular concretions and fibrous, and in 'cockscomb' masses, as well as earthy aggregates. Some 'desert roses' are formed from rosettes of baryte crystals enclosing sand grains. **Colour** Colourless to white, often yellow, blue, green, red, or brown (due to impurities of iron minerals); transparent to translucent. Vitreous lustre. White streak. **Occurrence** Most common barium mineral, found mainly as a gangue mineral in metalliferous hydrothermal veins, associated with ores of lead, copper, zinc, silver and iron, together with quartz, fluorite and dolomite. Also in residual surface deposits, in hot springs deposits and in cavities in some igneous rocks. Also occurs as a replacement deposit in limestones and as veins, cement or concretions in sedimentary rocks. Used primarily as a drilling mud for oil and gas wells. Also chief source of barium for chemicals. **Distinguishing properties** Habit; S.G. 4·5; hardness $3–3\frac{1}{2}$; perfect basal cleavage; prismatic, very good; uneven fracture. Insoluble in dilute acids. When powdered colours a flame apple-green (barium). Some specimens are fluorescent and phosphorescent in ultraviolet light.

Celestine

$SrSO_4$ Orthorhombic **Habit** Crystals tabular or elongated prismatic, similar to baryte; also fibrous, granular and concretionary masses. **Colour** Colourless, white, pale blue, sometimes red-brown; transparent to translucent. Vitreous lustre. White streak. **Occurrence** Chiefly occurs in sedimentary rocks, particularily in dolomite. Associated with baryte, gypsum, halite, dolomite and fluorite. Occurs also with anhydrite in evaporite deposits. Often found associated with sulphur in some volcanic areas. Occurs as a gangue mineral in hydrothermal veins with galena and sphalerite. **Distinguishing properties** Habit; S.G. 3·9–4·0; hardness 3–3½; perfect basal and good prismatic cleavage; uneven fracture. Insoluble in dilute acids. Colours a flame crimson (strontium).

Anglesite

$PbSO_4$ Orthorhombic **Habit** Crystals often tabular, sometimes elongated prismatic or pyramidal; also massive, compact and granular. Concentrically banded massive varieties sometimes enclose an unaltered core of galena. **Colour** Colourless to white, grey, pale shades of yellow, blue or green; transparent to opaque. Adamantine lustre when pure. White streak. **Occurrence** Common secondary mineral, most commonly found in the oxidized zone of lead deposits associated with galena, cerussite and other secondary lead minerals and silver halides. **Distinguishing properties** Lustre; association with galena; S.G. 6·2–6·4; hardness 3; good basal and distinct prismatic cleavage; conchoidal fracture. Does not effervesce in acids. Small fragments will fuse in a candle flame.

Anhydrite

$CaSO_4$ Orthorhombic **Habit** Crystals not common; usually massive, fibrous or granular. Sometimes as contorted concretionary forms. **Colour** Colourless or white when pure, often grey or reddish, frequently shows a bluish tinge; transparent to translucent. Vitreous to pearly lustre on cleavage. White streak. **Occurrence** Important rock forming mineral, found in bedded evaporite deposits. May be deposited directly from sea-water or formed by the dehydration of gypsum. Also found as a product of hydrothermal alteration of limestones and dolomites, or as a gangue mineral in hydrothermal metallic-ore veins **Distinguishing properties** S.G. 2·9–3·0; hardness 3–3½; three good pinacoidal cleavages at right angles, forming rectangular cleavage fragments; uneven fracture. Does not dissolve readily in dilute acids.

Gypsum

$CaSO_4.2H_2O$ Monoclinic **Habit** Crystals usually simple in habit; prismatic, tabular parallel to side, pinacoid often with curved faces; also granular, massive fibrous (satin spar). The fine grained granular variety is called alabaster. Twinning is very common, giving 'swallow-tail' or 'arrow-head' types as well as simple twins, often in radiating interpenetrating groups. **Colour** Colourless to white (colourless transparent variety is selenite), grey, sometimes yellow or brownish; transparent to translucent. Vitreous lustre, pearly parallel to cleavage. White streak. **Occurrence** Gypsum is found in extensive sedimentary deposits usually interbedded with limestones, sandstones and halite. As such it is the first salt precipitated from an evaporating brine, and is followed by anhydrite and halite. Also formed as a secondary mineral deposited from percolating ground-waters replacing other sedimentary rocks (some 'desert roses' are gypsum crystal rosettes enclosing sand

grains). Fine solitary crystals are found in some calcareous muds or clays in association with the decomposition of pyrite. Also occurs where a limestone has reacted with volcanic vapours, and as a gangue mineral in metallic veins. Used in the production of plaster of Paris and as a filler. **Distinguishing properties** Habit; S.G. 2·3; Hardness 2 (can be scratched with fingernail); one perfect cleavage, yielding thin flexible plates and two other distinct cleavages giving rhombic fragments. Dissolves in hot dilute hydrochloric acid.

Epsomite (Epsom Salt)

$MgSO_4.7H_2O$ Orthorhombic   **Habit** Rarely found as natural crystals; usually in botryoidal masses and fibrous crusts. **Colour** Colourless to white; transparent to translucent. Vitreous lustre, fibrous types silky to earthy. White streak. **Occurrence** As encrusting masses on the walls of caves and mine workings, where rocks rich in magnesium have been exposed. Also formed from some mineral waters and in volcanic fumaroles. **Distinguishing properties** Fibrous habit; occurrence; S.G. 1·7; hardness $3\frac{1}{2}$–4; one perfect cleavage; conchoidal fracture. Readily soluble in water, bitter taste.

Alunite

$KAL_3(SO_4)_2(OH)_6$ Hexagonal (Trigonal) **Habit** As small rare crystals with the rhombohedra and basal pinacoid present giving pseudocubic appearance; usually massive **Colour** White, sometimes grey, yellow or reddish; transparent to translucent. Vitreous to pearly lustre. White streak. **Occurrence** Alunite is usually found as a secondary mineral in near surface rocks of volcanic regions, which have been altered by solutions bearing sulphuric acid. **Distinguishing properties** S.G. 2·6–2·8; hardness $3\frac{1}{2}$–4; distinct basal cleavage; conchoidal fracture (crystals); uneven, splintery fracture (masses). Insoluble in water and practically insoluble in acids (slowly dissolves in sulphuric acid). Infusible. Difficult to distinguish from massive anhydrite, dolomite or magnesite without chemical or X-ray tests.

Jarosite (illustrated)

$KFe_3(SO_4)_2(OH)_6$ Hexagonal (Trigonal) **Habit** As crusts or coatings of minute tabular or pseudocubic rhombohedral crystals; also granular, massive, fibrous nodular and earthy. **Colour** Yellow ochre to dark brown. Vitreous to resinous lustre. Pale-yellow streak. **Occurrence** As coatings on and associated with iron ores. Found as a constituent of limonitic gossans. **Distinguishing properties** S.G. 3·0–3·2; hardness $2\frac{1}{2}$–$3\frac{1}{2}$; distinct basal cleavage; uneven fracture.

Plumbojarosite

$PbFe_6(SO_4)_4(OH)_{12}$ Hexagonal (Trigonal) **Habit** Minute tabular crystals; compact masses, also earthy. **Colour** Dark brown. Dull to glistening lustre. Brown streak. **Occurrence** Secondary mineral found in the oxidized zones of lead deposits. **Distinguishing properties** Habit; colour; associations; S.G. 3·67; hardness soft (talc-like).

Linarite

$(Pb,Cu)_2SO_4(OH)_2$ Monoclinic **Habit**
Commonly prismatic, also tabular,
either as single crystals or as groups
and crusts of radiating aggregates.
Twinning is common. **Colour** Deep
blue; translucent. Vitreous lustre, pale-
blue streak. **Occurrence** A rare but
distinctive secondary mineral, found
in the oxidized zone of some lead-
copper ores. **Distinguishing properties**
Colour; association; S.G. 5·3—5·4;
hardness $2\frac{1}{2}$—3; perfect pinacoidal,
distinct basal cleavage; conchoidal
fracture. Distinguished from azurite by
the lack of effervescence with dilute
hydrochloric acid.

Brochantite

$Cu_4SO_4(OH)_6$ Monoclinic **Habit**
Crystals are stout prismatic to acicular,
also tabular. Commonly as drusy crusts
and aggregates of crystals, massive,
granular. Twinning is common, forming
pseudo-orthorhombic forms. **Colour**
Emerald-green to blackish-green, pale
green; transparent to translucent. Vitreous lustre, pearly on cleavage. Pale-
green streak. **Occurrence** As a
secondary mineral in the oxidized zone
of copper deposits, especially in arid
regions, but of worldwide occurrence.
Distinguishing properties Colour;
habit; association; S.G. 4·0; hardness
$3\frac{1}{2}$—4; perfect cleavage; conchoidal to
uneven fracture. Soluble in hydrochloric and nitric acids.

Crocoite

$PbCrO_4$ Monoclinic **Habit** Usually prismatic or acicular crystals, often striated, with brilliant faces, crystals sometimes hollow; also massive columnar or granular. **Colour** Bright orange-red, various shades to brown; translucent. Adamantine to vitreous lustre. Orange-yellow streak. **Occurrence** A rare secondary mineral found in the oxidized zone of lead-chromium veins, together with other secondary lead minerals such as cerussite and pyromorphite. **Distinguishing properties** Habit; colour and lustre; S.G. 5·9–6·1; hardness $2\frac{1}{2}$–3; distinct prismatic cleavage; conchoidal to uneven fracture. Easily fusible.

Wolframite

$(Fe,Mn)WO_4$ Monoclinic. Virtually a complete substitution series exists from ferberite $(FeWO_4)$ to hubnerite $(MnWO_4)$. **Habit** Crystals tabular or prismatic to long prismatic. Often forms bladed, striated subparallel groups; also found massive, granular. Common as simple contact twins. **Colour** hubnerite is reddish brown to brownish black, wolframite is brownish black, ferberite is black; translucent to opaque. Generally sub-metallic lustre. Reddish-brown to brownish-black streak. **Occurrence** Found in quartz veins and pegmatites associated with metallic ores. Also found in high-temperature hydrothermal veins. Occurs in some alluvial deposits. **Distinguishing properties** Colour; S.G. 7·0–7·5 (increases with iron content); hardness 4–$4\frac{1}{2}$; one perfect cleavage; uneven fracture. Ferberite is weakly magnetic.

Scheelite

$CaWO_4$ Tetragonal **Habit** Crystals usually bipyramidal, often with striated faces, sometime tabular; also massive, granular. Twinning is common, usually as penetration twins. **Colour** Colourless to white, usually pale yellow, also greenish, grey, brownish or reddish (coloured tints usually due to molybdenum content); transparent to translucent. Vitreous to adamantine lustre. White streak. **Occurrence** Often accompanies wolframite in pegmatites and high-temperature hydrothermal veins. Associated with cassiterite, molybdenite, fluorite and topaz. Also found in some contact metamorphic deposits with garnet, axinite, idocrase and wollastonite. **Distinguishing properties** Pyramidal habit; colour; S.G. 5·9–6·1; hardness 4½–5; good pyramidal cleavage; uneven fracture. Most scheelite will fluoresce under ultraviolet light.

Wulfenite

$PbMoO_4$ Tetragonal **Habit** Crystals usually square tabular plates, sometimes very thin, short prismatic or stubby, more rarely bipyramidal; also massive, coarse to fine granular. **Colour** Yellow, orange-red, grey, white, olive-green to brown, transparent to translucent. Vitreous to adamantine lustre. White streak. **Occurrence** Found as a secondary mineral formed in the oxidized zone of deposits of lead and molybdenum minerals, commonly associated with vanadinite, cerussite, anglesite and pyromorphite. **Distinguishing properties** Tabular crystals; colour and lustre; association; S.G. 6·5–7·0; hardness 3; distinct pyramidal cleavage; subconchoidal to uneven fracture. Fuses readily.

Phosphates and Arsenates
Xenotime

YPO_4 Tetragonal. Other rare-earth elements may substitute for yttrium. **Habit** Crystals short to long prismatic, also equant and pyramidal, closely resembling zircon with which it is often found in parallel growth. Sometimes occurs as radial aggregates of coarse crystals. **Colour** Yellow to reddish-brown, also greyish-white, pale yellow; translucent to opaque. Resinous to vitreous lustre. Pale-brown streak. **Occurrence** As a minor accessory mineral in granite and alkaline igneous rocks occurring as larger crystals in the associated pegmatites. Also occurs in some gneisses. **Distinguishing properties** Crystal form; S.G. 4·4–5·1; hardness 4–5 (c.p. zircon $7\frac{1}{2}$); perfect prismatic cleavage; uneven fracture.

Monazite

$(Ce, La, Th)PO_4$ Monoclinic **Habit** Crystals usually small, often tabular or short prismatic. Faces are sometimes rough, uneven and striated. Twinning is common, both as contact and penetration (cruciform) twins. **Colour** Yellowish- or reddish-brown to brown, also green; subtranslucent to subtransparent. Resinous to waxy lustre. Streak is white or pale shades of above. **Occurrence** As an accessory mineral in granitic and associated pegmatitic rocks Also in gneissic metamorphic rocks. Detrital sands derived from these rocks often contain considerable, commercial quantities of monazite. **Distinguishing properties** Crystal form; S.G. 4·6–5·4 (mostly around 5); hardness 5–$5\frac{1}{2}$; distinct pinacoidal cleavage also basal parting; uneven fracture. Infusible.

Vivianite

$Fe_3(PO_4)_2.8H_2O$ Monoclinic **Habit** Crystals usually prismatic, sometimes flattened and blade-like in radiating groups; also as reniform or encrusting masses often with a fibrous structure. Sometimes powdery and earthy. **Colour** Colourless and transparent when fresh, becoming green, pale to dark blue by oxidation; transparent to translucent. Vitreous lustre, pearly parallel to cleavage. White or pale-blue streak, rapidly changing to dark blue or brown. **Occurrence** As a secondary mineral in the oxidized zone of metallic ore deposits containing iron sulphides also in weathered zones of phosphate-rich pegmatites, and in sedimentary rocks especially those containing organic matter. **Distinguishing properties** Colour and streak; S.G. 2.6–2.7; hardness $1\frac{1}{2}$–2; one perfect cleavage, thin cleavage plates flexible. Easily soluble in acids.

Amblygonite

$(Li,Na)Al(PO_4)(F,OH)$ Triclinic **Habit** As small crystals which are short prismatic to equant, larger crystals rough and ill-formed; also massive, compact, commonly as cleavable masses. Lamellar twinning common. **Colour** White to creamy white, also pale shades of green, blue, pink or yellow; translucent to transparent. Vitreous to greasy lustre. White streak. **Occurrence** Found in granite pegmatites together with other lithium-and phosphate-rich minerals. **Distinguishing properties** Association; S.G. 3·1; hardness $5\frac{1}{2}$–6; one perfect and one good cleavage; Uneven to subconchoidal fracture. Not easily soluble in acids. Fragments fuse easily and colour a flame red (lithium). Varieties in which hydroxyl is in excess of fluorine are common and are called montebrasite.

Apatite

$Ca_5(PO_4)_3(F,Cl,OH)$ Hexagonal **Habit**
Crystals common, short to long prismatic, sometimes tabular; also massive, granular. Occasionally globular or reniform, earthy or nodular. **Colour** Usually in shades of green to grey-green, also white, blue, green, violet, or reddish; transparent to translucent. Vitreous lustre. White streak. **Occurrence** An accessory mineral in a wide range of igneous rocks, including pegmatites and high-temperature hydrothermal veins, in both regional and contact metamorphic rocks especially in metamorphosed limestones. Also in sedimentary rocks as bedded marine-deposits. Apatite is the principal inorganic constituent of bone and teeth. **Distinguishing properties** Habit; S.G. 3·1–3·3; hardness 5; imperfect basal cleavage; conchoidal to uneven fracture. Dissolves in hydrochloric acid.

Pyromorphite

$Pb_5(PO_4)_3Cl$ Hexagonal. Arsenic substitutes for phosphorous and a complete series extends to mimetite. **Habit** Crystals usually of simple prismatic form, often in rounded barrel-shaped forms (campylite); also hollow; often globular, reniform, granular. **Colour** Various shades of green and brown, also orange-yellow and red, rarely colourless; subtransparent to translucent. Resinous to adamantine lustre. White or yellowish-white streak. **Occurrence** A secondary mineral found in the oxidized zone of lead deposits, associated with other lead minerals. Crystals are sometimes zoned with the outer parts tending to mimetite. **Distinguishing properties** Habit; colour and lustre; S.G. 6·5–7·1; hardness $3\frac{1}{2}$–4; poor prismatic cleavage; subconchoidal to uneven fracture. Dissolves in hydrochloric and nitric acids.

Mimetite

$Pb_5(AsO_4)_3Cl$ Hexagonal **Habit** Crystals are similar to those of pyromorphite, commonly simple hexagonal forms of prismatic habit, also as the curved barrel-shaped crystals, also globular (campylite); sometimes as botryoidal crusts. **Colour** Pale yellow to yellow-brown, orange-yellow; transparent to translucent. Resinous to adamantine lustre. White streak. **Occurrence** As a secondary mineral occurring in the oxidized zone of arsenic-bearing lead-deposits often associated with pyromorphite, galena, anglesite and hemimorphite. **Distinguishing properties** Crystal form; colour and lustre; S.G. 7·0–7·2; hardness $3\frac{1}{2}$–4; subconchoidal fracture. Dissolves in hydrochloric acid. Difficult to distinguish from pyromorphite without chemical tests.

Vanadinite

$Pb_5(VO_4)_3Cl$ Hexagonal **Habit** Crystals are usually short to long prismatic, also acicular, sometimes as hollow prisms; also as rounded forms, globules and in subparallel groupings. **Colour** Orange-red, brownish-red to shades of brown and yellow; subtransparent to nearly opaque. Resinous lustre. White to yellowish streak. **Occurrence** As a secondary mineral found in the oxidized zone of ore deposits containing galena and other sulphides. It is found associated with pyromorphite, wulfenite, cerussite, anglesite and linarite. **Distinguishing properties** Habit; Colour and lustre; S.G. 6·7–7·1; hardness 3; uneven to conchoidal fracture. Easily fusible. Dissolves in hydrochloric acid giving a green solution with a whitish precipitate.

Turquoise

$CuAl_6(PO_4)_4(OH)_8.5H_2O$ Triclinic
Habit Crystals are very rare, minute; usually massive, cryptocrystalline to fine-granular, as veinlets and crusts, stalactitic or concretionary shapes. **Colour** Sky-blue, bluish-green to apple-green; transparent (crystals), to nearly opaque. Vitreous lustre (crystals) to waxy (massive). White or pale-green streak. **Occurrence** As a secondary mineral formed by the action of surface waters, usually in arid regions, on a aluminous igneous and sedimentary rocks. Usually forming in veins or irregular patches in the rock. **Distinguishing properties** Habit; colour; S.G. 2·6–2·8; hardness 5–6 (harder than chrysocolla); two good cleavages in crystals; massive material has a conchoidal fracture. It is fusible.

Erythrite (cobalt bloom) (illustrated) and Annabergite (nickel bloom)

$Co_3(AsO_4)_2.8H_2O$ and
$Ni_3(AsO_4)_2.8H_2O$ Monoclinic. Cobalt and nickel substitute for one another to form a complete composition series. **Habit** Crystals are usually prismatic, often acicular and flattened, sometimes deeply striated and as radiating groups. Commonly as globular or reniform shapes, earthy or powdery. **Colour** Erythrite, crimson-red and pink (illustrated above); Annabergite, apple-green; transparent to translucent. Adamantine to dull lustre. Streak is as colour but paler. **Occurrence** Secondary minerals produced by the surface oxidation of cobalt and nickel arsenides in some ore deposits. **Distinguishing properties** Colour; association with other cobalt-nickel minerals is distinctive; S.G. 3·0–3·1; Hardness $1\frac{1}{2}$–$2\frac{1}{2}$; one perfect cleavage. Dissolves in acids.

Scorodite

$FeAsO_4 \cdot 2H_2O$ Orthorhombic **Habit** Crystals usually pyramidal and pseudo-octahedral, also tabular or prismatic, often forming crusts; also massive nodular or earthy. **Colour** Pale green, blue-green to blue, brown; transparent to translucent. Vitreous to adamantine lustre. White streak. **Occurrence** Usually found as a secondary mineral in gossans formed by the alteration of arsenic minerals, especially arseno-pyrite. **Distinguishing properties** Habit; association with arsenic minerals; S.G. $3 \cdot 1 - 3 \cdot 3$; hardness $3\frac{1}{2} - 4$; imperfect prismatic cleavage; sub-conchoidal fracture. Dissolves in hydrochloric and nitric acids.

Torbernite (illustrated) and Metatorbernite

$Cu(UO_2)_2(PO_4)_2 \cdot 8 - 12H_2O$ Tetragonal. At atmospheric temperatures torbernite loses some of its water and tends to form metatorbernite. **Habit** Crystals are often square, thin to thick tabular; also as foliated or scaly aggregates. **Colour** Bright emerald-green to grass-green; transparent to translucent. Vitreous lustre, pearly parallel to cleavage. Streak is paler than colour. **Occurrence** Found as a secondary mineral in the oxidized zone of veins containing copper minerals and uraninite usually associated with other secondary uranium minerals. **Distinguishing properties** Crystal form; colour; S.G. $3 \cdot 2$ (torbernite) increasing to $3 \cdot 7$ (metatorbernite); hardness $2 - 2\frac{1}{2}$; perfect basal cleavage, producing thin brittle cleavage plates. Dissolves in hydrochloric and nitric acids. Does not fluoresce.

Autunite (Meta-autunite)

$Ca(UO_2)(PO_4)_2.10–12H_2O$ Tetragonal
Habit Crystals occur as square, thin to thick tabular crystals; also as foliated or scaly aggregates, sometimes forming thick crusts of subparallel crystals.
Colour Bright lemon to greenish yellow; transparent to translucent. Vitreous lustre. Yellow streak. **Occurrence** Found as a secondary mineral in the zone of oxidation and weathering, and hydrothermal veins and pegmatites rich in uraninite. **Distinguishing properties.** Crystal form; colour; S.G. 3·1–3·2; hardness 2–2½; perfect basal cleavage; producing thin cleavage plates less brittle than torbernite. Dissolves in hydrochloric and nitric acids. Fluoresces strongly (yellow-green) in ultraviolet light. Distinguished from yellow secondary uranium minerals by chemical or X-ray methods. Radioactive.

Carnotite

$K_2(UO_2)_2(VO_4)_2.3H_2O$ Monoclinic
Habit Rarely as minute, thin tabular crystals, usually as powdery or loose microcrystalline aggregates, sometimes compact. **Colour** Bright yellow to greenish yellow. Dull, earthy lustre. **Occurrence** As a secondary mineral formed from circulating ground waters which have passed through ore deposits containing uranium and vanadium minerals, generally disseminated through sandstones. Also found as an alteration crust on some uranium ores. **Distinguishing properties** Powdery habit; colour; S.G. 5 (when fully hydrated); hardness about 2; perfect basal cleavage. Easily dissolves in hydrochloric and nitric acids. Does not fluoresce (compare autunite).

Descloizite

$Pb(Zn,Cu)VO_4(OH)$ Orthorhombic. A compositional series exists due to substitution of copper for zinc to mottramite $(Pb(Cu,Zn)VO_4(OH))$. **Habit** Crystals are prismatic, tabular or wedge-shaped, faces are usually uneven or rough, subparallel growth is common. Occurs commonly as crystalline crusts; also mamillated with fibrous radiating structure. **Colour** Brownish red to blackish brown, also orange-red to nearly black; transparent to opaque. Greasy lustre. Orange to brownish-red streak. **Occurrence** A secondary mineral occasionally found in the oxidized zone of some lead-zinc deposits. **Distinguishing properties** Crystal form; colour and streak; S.G. 5·9 (mottramite)—6.2 (descloizite); hardness 3—4; uneven fracture. Easily dissolves in hydrochloric or nitric acids.

Olivenite

$Cu_2AsO_4(OH)$ Orthorhombic **Habit** Crystals prismatic or acicular, often elongated, frequently occurs as globular and reniform shapes with a radiating fibrous internal structure, also massive, granular to earthy. **Colour** Shades of olive-green to brown, but also paler shades to greyish white; translucent to opaque. Adamantine to vitreous lustre. Olive-green to brown streak. **Occurrence** As a secondary mineral found in the oxidized zone of copper sulphide deposits, associated with other copper minerals. **Distinguishing properties** Habit; colour and streak; S.G. 4·1—4·5; hardness 3; poor cleavage; conchoidal to irregular fracture. Dissolves in hydrochloric and nitric acids.

Libethenite

$Cu_2PO_4(OH)$ Orthorhombic **Habit** Crystals are short prismatic or equant; commonly composite and forming crusts. **Colour** Light to dark olive-green; transparent to translucent. Vitreous lustre. **Occurrence** A secondary mineral found in the oxidized zone of copper ore deposits, associated with other primary and secondary copper minerals. **Distinguishing properties** Colour; association; S.G. 3·9; hardness 4; very poor cleavage; conchoidal to uneven fracture. Easily dissolves in hydrochloric and nitric acids. Can be easily confused with olivenite.

Adamite

$Zn_2AsO_4(OH)$ Orthorhombic Copper may substitute for zinc to a considerable extent (cuproadamite). **Habit** Crystals usually small, and merged together in crusts or as roughly radial aggregates. **Colour** Commonly yellowish-green, to brownish-yellow, copper-bearing varieties are shades of green, cobalt-bearing varieties violet-rose; transparent to translucent. Vitreous lustre. **Occurrence** A secondary mineral, found in the oxidized zone of ore deposits, containing primary zinc and arsenic-rich minerals. Often encrusting limonite. **Distinguishing properties** Colour; S.G. 4·3–4·4; hardness $3\frac{1}{2}$; one good cleavage; uneven to subconchoidal fracture. Easily dissolved in dilute acids. Some specimens fluoresce lemon-yellow in ultra-violet light.

Liroconite

$Cu_2Al(AsO_4)(OH)_4.4H_2O$ Monoclinic
Habit Crystals are thin and wedge-shaped, with some faces striated, often as subparallel groups, also coarsely granular. **Colour** Sky blue to green; transparent to translucent. Vitreous to resinous lustre. Streak is paler than its colour. **Occurrence** A rare secondary mineral found in the oxidized zone of copper deposits associated with azurite, malachite, cuprite, olivenite, chalcophyllite and limonite. **Distinguishing properties** Colour and association; S.G. 2·9–3·0; hardness 2–2½; indistinct cleavage; conchoidal to uneven fracture. Easily dissolves in hydrochloric and nitric acids.

Chalcophyllite

$Cu_{18}Al_2(AsO_4)_3(SO_4)_3(OH)_{27}.33H_2O$
Habit Crystals are thin tabular, six-sided forms; sometimes striated; also as foliated masses or rosettes. **Colour** Emerald green, also bluish-green; transparent to translucent. Vitreous to adamantine lustre. Pale-green streak. **Occurrence** As a rare secondary mineral in the oxidization zone of copper-bearing ore deposits associated with other copper minerals. **Distinguishing properties** Habit and colour; S.G. 2·6–2·7; hardness 2; perfect basal cleavage, forming flexible cleavage plates. Dissolves in hydrochloric and nitric acids. Alters readily to chrysocolla.

Lazulite

$(Mg,Fe)Al_2(PO_4)_2(OH)_2$ Monoclinic
Scorzalite is a related mineral but with
iron predominating over magnesium.
Habit Crystals are commonly steep
pyramidal; also massive, compact to
granular. Twinning is common. **Colour**
Deep azure-blue, also paler shades of
blue; translucent. (gem varieties are
transparent). Vitreous lustre. White
streak. **Occurrence** A rare mineral
found in some metamorphic rocks, as
grains or masses especially in quartzites, also in granite-pegmatite. Found
associated with high-grade metamorphic minerals such as kyanite,
sillimanite, corundum, muscovite and
garnet. **Distinguishing properties**
Crystal form; colour; association; S.G.
3.1; hardness $5\frac{1}{2}$–6; indistinct prismatic
cleavage; uneven to splintery fracture.
Lazulite is much more common than
scorzalite.

Wavellite

$Al_3(PO_4)_2(OH)_3.5H_2O$ Orthorhombic
Habit Crystals are rare, usually occurs
as hemispherical or globular aggregates
with a fibrous radiating internal structure; also as crusts or stalactites.
Colour Colourless to white, yellow,
green and brown; translucent. Vitreous lustre. White streak. **Occurrence**
As a secondary mineral found on
joint surfaces and in cavities of low
grade metamorphic rocks such as
slates and in some sedimentary phosphate rock deposits. Sometimes found
in limonitic-ore bodies. **Distinguishing
properties** Habit; S.G. 2.3–2.4; hardness $3\frac{1}{2}$–4; good prismatic cleavage;
uneven to subconchoidal fracture.
Easily dissolves in most acids.

Childrenite

$(Fe,Mn)Al(PO_4)(OH)_2.H_2O$ Ortho-rhombic **Habit** Crystals equant or pyramidal to short prismatic (manganese—rich variety, eosphorite: long prismatic); also thick tabular, sometimes platy. **Colour** Brown to yellowish-brown. Rose-red (eosphorite); transparent to translucent. Vitreous to resinous lustre. White streak. **Occurrence** A rare mineral, but sometimes found as fine crystals in some hydrothermal vein deposits and in granite pegmatites. **Distinguishing properties** Habit; colour; S.G. 3·2–3·3 (childrenite) 3·0–3·1 (eosphorite); hardness 5; poor cleavage; subconchoidal to uneven fracture.

Ludlamite

$Fe_3(PO_4)_2.4H_2O$ Monoclinic **Habit** Thin to thick tabular crystals, sometimes wedge-shaped; also massive, granular. **Colour** Bright green to apple green; translucent. Vitreous lustre. Greenish-white streak. **Occurrence** As a secondary mineral in the oxidation zone of ore deposits and as an alteration product of primary iron phosphate minerals in some granite pegmatites, often associated with vivianite **Distinguishing properties** Colour; S.G. 3·1–3·2; hardness $3\frac{1}{2}$; perfect cleavage.

Variscite and Strengite

$Al(PO_4).2H_2O$ and $Fe(PO_4).2H_2O$ Orthorhombic **Habit** Crystals rare, usually as nodules and crusts. **Colour** Variscite — various shades of green. Strengite — red or violet. White streak. **Occurrence** Secondary phosphate minerals found in near-surface deposits. **Distinguishing properties** Colour; variscite from Fairfield, Utah; forms characteristic nodules.

Silicates

The silicate minerals constitute almost a third of known mineral species and form over 90% of the Earth's crust. The feldspar minerals and quartz are the most common minerals in the Earth's crust.

Willemite

Zn_2SiO_4 Hexagonal (Trigonal) **Habit** Found as small prismatic or rhombohedral crystals; usually massive, granular. **Colour** Commonly pale greenish-yellow but varies from near white to dark brown; transparent to nearly opaque. Vitreous to resinous lustre. White streak. **Occurrence** Found in the oxidized zone of some zinc-ore deposits. Abundant in the ore deposit at Franklin, New Jersey, U.S.A. **Distinguishing properties** Colour; association; S.G. 3·9–4·2; hardness $5\frac{1}{2}$; good basal cleavage. Willemite often shows strong fluorescence in ultraviolet light.

Phenakite

Be_2SiO_4 Hexagonal (Trigonal) **Habit** Crystals are often rhombohedral or prismatic; also granular, and as acicular, columnar aggregates. Twinning is common. **Colour** Colourless, also white, yellow, pink and brown; transparent to translucent. Vitreous lustre. **Occurrence** A rare beryllium mineral found in cavities in granite and granitic pegmatites in association with beryl, topaz and apatite, also found in some hydrothermal veins. **Distinguishing properties** Crystal form; S.G. 3·0; hardness $7\frac{1}{2}$–8; distinct prismatic cleavage; conchoidal fracture.

Olivine

$(Mg,Fe)_2SiO_4$ Orthorhombic   A continuous solid solution series exists between two components Mg_2SiO_4 (forsterite) and Fe_2SiO_4 (fayalite). **Habit**   Well-developed crystals rare, usually occurs in granular masses or as isolated grains. **Colour** Olive-green, also white (forsterite) and brown to black (fayalite); transparent to translucent. Vitreous lustre. White or grey streak.   **Occurrence**   A rock forming mineral, typical of basalt, gabbro and peridotite. Dunite is composed entirely of olivine. Basalts occasionally contain nodules of granular olivine and pyroxene. Forsteritic olivines are formed during the metamorphism of magnesium-rich sediments. Fayalite occurs in some pitchstones and slags.   **Distinguishing properties**   Colour; association; S.G. 3·2 (forsterite)—4·4 (fayalite); hardness $6\frac{1}{2}$—7; indistinct pinacoidal cleavage; conchoidal fracture.

Humite Series

$Mg(OH,F)_2.1–4Mg_2SiO_4$ Orthorhombic and monoclinic   The group comprises four minerals, norbergite, chondrodite, humite and clinohumite. They differ in the amount of magnesia and silica they contain. Humite and norbergite are orthorhombic, chondrodite and clinohumite are monoclinic. **Habit** Crystals are usually stubby, often highly modified; also massive. **Colour** White, pale yellow-brown; translucent. Vitreous to resinous lustre.   **Occurrence** Found typically in metamorphosed dolomite limestones in association with spinel, phlogopite, garnet, diopside and idocrase.   **Distinguishing properties**   Habit; colour; association with metamorphosed limestones; S.G. 3·1–3·3; hardness $6–6\frac{1}{2}$; One poor cleavage; uneven fracture.

Zircon

$ZrSiO_4$ Tetragonal **Habit** Crystals usually prismatic, with bipyramidal terminations. Twinning is common, forming knee-shaped twins. **Colour** Usually brown or reddish-brown, but sometimes found colourless, grey, green or violet; transparent to translucent. Vitreous to adamantine lustre. White streak. **Occurrence** A common accessory mineral in igneous rocks such as granite, syenite and nepheline syenites. In pegmatites, crystals sometimes reach a considerable size. Also found in metamorphic rocks such as schists and gneisses. Often as a detrital mineral in river and beach sands. **Distinguishing properties** Habit; colour; S.G. 4·6—4·7; hardness $7\frac{1}{2}$; indistinct prismatic cleavage; uneven to conchoidal fracture. Zircon is often radioactive due to thorium and uranium replacing zirconium.

Andalusite

Al_2SiO_5 Orthorhombic. Andalusite, sillimanite and kyanite are polymorphs of Al_2SiO_5. **Habit** Crystals prismatic, nearly square in cross-section; also massive. The variety chiastolite exhibits a cruciform pattern of carbonaceous impurities when viewed in cross-section. **Colour** Commonly pink or red, also grey, yellow, brown and green; transparent to nearly opaque. Vitreous lustre. White streak. **Occurrence** Found typically in thermally metamorphosed argillaceous schists and in regionally metamorphosed rocks formed under low pressure conditions. Rarely found in some granite pegmatites. **Distinguishing properties** Habit; association; S.G. 3·1—3·2; hardness $6\frac{1}{2}$—$7\frac{1}{2}$; distinct prismatic cleavage; uneven to subconchoidal fracture. Readily alters to an aggregate of white mica flakes which coat crystals.

Sillimanite (Fibrolite)

Al_2SiO_5 Orthorhombic **Habit** Commonly occurs as elongated prismatic crystals, striated along their length, often as fibrous or interwoven masses. **Colour** Colourless or white, yellow-brown or greenish; transparent to translucent. Vitreous lustre, often silky in fibrous material. White streak. **Occurrence** Found typically in schists and gneisses produced by high-grade regional metamorphism. **Distinguishing properties** Fibrous habit resembling other fibrous silicates such as wollastonite and tremolite. For precise identification optical or X-ray tests are needed. S.G. 3·2–3·3: hardness $6\frac{1}{2}–7\frac{1}{2}$; perfect prismatic cleavage. Infusible and insoluble in acids.

Kyanite (Disthene)

Al_2SiO_5 Triclinic **Habit** Crystals usually flat and bladed, seldom terminated; also as radiating, bladed aggregates. Crystals are distinctly flexible and often bent or twisted. **Colour** Commonly blue to white but may be grey or green, often a patchy blue; transparent to translucent. Vitreous lustre, sometimes pearly on cleavage surfaces. White streak. **Occurrence** Typically found in medium to high-grade regionally metamorphosed schists and gneisses; associated with garnet, staurolite, mica and quartz. Also occurs in some pegmatites and quartz veins associated with schists and gneisses. **Distinguishing properties** Habit; colour; S.G. 3·5–3·7; hardness variable, $5\frac{1}{2}$ along the length of the crystals and 6–7 across; one perfect and one good cleavage; also a basal parting.

Staurolite

$(Fe,Mg)_2(Al,Fe)_9Si_4O_{22}(O,OH)_2$
Monoclinic (pseudo-orthorhombic)
Habit Usually as prismatic crystals, often with rough surfaces; rarely massive. Twinning is common, as cruciform twins, forming crosses near 90° and also oblique crosses at about 60°.
Colour Reddish-brown to brownblack; translucent to nearly opaque. Vitreous to resinous lustre. Grey streak.
Occurrence Typically found as porphyroblasts in medium-grade aluminium-rich schists and gneisses, often in association with garnet, kyanite and mica. **Distinguishing properties** Habit, (particularly if twinned); colour; S.G. 3·7–3·8; hardness 7–7½; distinct cleavage; uneven to subconchoidal fracture.

Ilvaite (illustrated)

$CaFe^{2+}_2Fe^{3+}Si_2O_8(OH)$ Orthorhombic
Habit Crystals prismatic, often diamond-shaped in cross-section, striated along the length; also columnar or massive. **Colour** Black; opaque. Dull submetallic lustre. Black streak.
Occurrence Found chiefly as a contact metasomatic mineral, in iron-, zinc- and copper-ore deposits. **Distinguishing properties** Habit and streak; S.G. 3·8–4·1; hardness 5½–6; distinct basal cleavage; uneven fracture.

Bertrandite

$H_2Be_4Si_2O_9$ Orthorhombic **Habit** Small tabular or prismatic crystals. Heart-shaped twins. **Colour** Colourless to pale yellow. **Occurrence** Found in pegmatites associated with beryl. **Distinguishing properties** Habit; association; S.G. 2·6; hardness 6–7; prismatic cleavage.

Topaz

$Al_2SiO_4(OH,F)_2$ Orthorhombic **Habit** As well-developed short to long prismatic crystals, sometimes striated; often with well-developed terminations; also massive, granular. **Colour** Colourless or white, pale blue and yellow, yellow-brown, rarely pink; transparent to translucent. Vitreous lustre. White streak. **Occurrence** Typically found in granite pegmatites, high-temperature quartz veins, and rhyolites. As grains in granites which have been altered by fluorine-rich solutions and characteristically associated with fluorite, tourmaline, apatite, beryl and cassiterite. Also as rounded grains or pebbles in alluvial deposits. **Distinguishing properties** Habit; S.G. 3·5–3·6; hardness 8; perfect basal cleavage; subconchoidal to uneven fracture.

Euclase (illustrated)

$BeAlSiO_4(OH)$ Monoclinic **Habit** Usually found as prismatic crystals. **Colour** Colourless to pale blue-green; transparent to translucent. Vitreous lustre. **Occurrence** A rare mineral found in pegmatites in association with beryl. **Distinguishing properties** Habit; colour; association; S.G. 3·0–3·1; hardness $7\frac{1}{2}$; one perfect cleavage.

Gadolinite

$Be_2Fe(YO)_2(SiO_4)_2$ Monoclinic. Other rare earth elements substitute for yttrium. **Habit** Prismatic crystals but usually massive. **Colour** Black, sometimes brown; vitreous lustre. **Occurrence** In pegmatite veins, frequently associated with allanite. **Distinguishing properties** Colour; habit and association; S.G. 4–4·5; hardness 6·5–7.

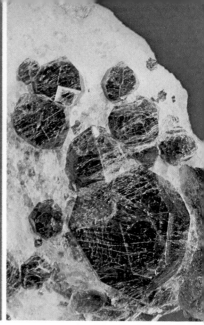

Sphene (Titanite)

$CaTiSiO_5$ Monoclinic **Habit** Crystals commonly flattened and wedge-shaped, also massive. Twinning is common, forming contact or cruciform penetration twins. **Colour** Brown and yellowish-green common, green to grey; transparent to nearly opaque. Resinous to adamantine lustre. White streak. **Occurrence** Widely distributed as an accessory mineral in intermediate and acid igneous rocks and associated pegmatites. Also in schists, gneisses and some metamorphosed limestones. Rarely as a detrital mineral in sediments. **Distinguishing properties** S.G. 3·4–3·6; hardness 5–5½; prismatic distinct cleavage; conchoidal fracture. Sharp, wedge-shaped habit, adamantine lustre and colour are particularly distinctive.

Garnet Group

Cubic. The garnets comprise a group of isomorphous minerals with the general formula $X_3Y_2Si_3O_{12}$ in which X may be Ca, Mn, Mg or Fe^{2+} and Y may be Al, Cr or Fe^{3+}. The following names are in common use: almandine $Fe_3Al_2Si_3O_{12}$); pyrope $(Mg_3Al_2 Si_3O_{12})$; spessartine $(Mn_3Al_2Si_3O_{12})$; grossular $(Ca_3Al_2Si_3O_{12})$; andradite $(Ca_3Fe_2Si_3O_{12})$; uvarovite $(Ca_3Cr_2 Si_3O_{12})$. Considerable atomic substitution may occur between these. **Habit** Crystals are common, usually rhombdodecahedral or icositetrahedral. Sometimes massive or granular. **Colour** Pyrope, almandine and spessartine are usually shades of deep-red and brown to nearly black; grossular is brown, pale green or white; andradite is yellow, brown or black; uvarovite is green. Transparent to translucent. Vitreous to resinous lustre. Normally white streak. **Occurrence** Pyrope occurs in ultrabasic igneous rocks such as peridotite, and high-grade, magnesium-rich metamorphic rocks. Almandine is the

Idocrase (Vesuvianite)

$Ca_{10}(Mg,Fe)_2Al_4(SiO_4)_5(Si_2O_7)_2(OH,F)_4$
Tetragonal **Habit** Mainly as short prismatic crystals, often with striations parallel to their length; also massive, granular or columnar. **Colour** Various shades of green, dark green, brown, white-yellow; blue varieties are called cyprine; transparent to translucent. Vitreous to resinous lustre. White streak. **Occurrence** Formed by the contact metamorphism of impure limestones; commonly associated with calcite, grossularite or andradite garnet and wollastonite. Often in blocks of limestone erupted from Mount Vesuvius. **Distinguishing properties** Prismatic, striated crystal form; S.G. 3·3–3·5; hardness 6–7; poor prismatic cleavage; uneven to conchoidal fracture.

common garnet of schists and gneisses. Spessartine occurs in low-grade metamorphic rocks. Uvarovite occurs in association with chromite in serpentinite. Grossular is formed by the contact or regional metamorphism of impure limestones. Andradite is commonly formed by the metasomatic alteration of limestones by iron-bearing solutions. The black variety, melanite (titanium andradite), occurs in some feldspathoidal igneous rocks. Also found as a constituent of beach and river sands. **Distinguishing properties** Habit; colour and mode of occurrence often indicate the garnet species present; S.G. 3·6–4·3 (varies with composition); hardness $6\frac{1}{2}$–$7\frac{1}{2}$; subconchoidal fracture. Chemical analysis normally required for precise composition. Some varieties cut as gemstones, mainly pyrope (red-brown).

Hemimorphite (Calamine)

$Zn_4Si_2O_7(OH)_2.H_2O$ Orthorhombic
Habit Crystals are tabular; also massive, fibrous or mamillated. **Colour** White, sometimes blue, greenish or brownish; transparent to translucent. Vitreous lustre. White streak. **Occurrence** A secondary mineral found in the oxidized zone of zinc-bearing ore bodies usually very close to the surface; also in limestones. Associated with galena, sphalerite, smithsonite, cerussite and anglesite. **Distinguishing properties** Crystal form; S.G. 3·4–3·5; hardness $4\frac{1}{2}$–5; perfect prismatic cleavage; conchoidal to uneven fracture. Soluble in hydrochloric acid but without effervescence. The name calamine is also often applied to smithsonite.

Epidote Group

The general formula is $X_2Y_3Si_3O_{12}(OH)$ in which X is commonly Ca, partly replaced by rare earth elements in allanite, and Y is Al and Fe^{3+} partly replaced by Mg and Fe^{2+} in allanite, and by Mn^{3+} in piemontite.

Zoisite

$Ca_2Al_3Si_3O_{12}(OH)$ Orthorhombic
Habit As aggregates of long prismatic crystals, often deeply striated commonly massive. **Colour** White, grey, greenish-brown, green, also pink (thulite), blue to purple (tanzanite); transparent to translucent. Vitreous lustre, pearly on cleavage surfaces. White to grey-white streak. **Occurrence** Found in schists and gneisses and in metasomatic rocks, together with garnet, idocrase and actinolite. Occasionally formed in hydrothermal veins. **Distinguishing properties** Colour; S.G. 3·2–3·4; hardness $6\frac{1}{2}$; perfect pinacoidal cleavage; uneven fracture.

Clinozoisite and Epidote (illustrated)

$Ca_2Al_3Si_3O_{12}(OH)$ and $Ca_2(Al,Fe)_3Si_3O_{12}(OH)$ Monoclinic **Habit** Crystals are prismatic, often deeply striated parallel to their length; mostly massive, granular or fibrous. Twinning is lamellar, but not common. **Colour** Pale green, or greenish-grey (clinozoisite); yellowish-green to black (epidote); transparent to nearly opaque. Vitreous lustre. White, grey-white streak. **Occurrence** Common in low-medium grade metamorphic rocks, also from calcareous sediments. Found in veins in igneous rocks. **Distinguishing properties** Habit; colour; S.G. 3·2–3·5; hardness 6–7; one perfect cleavage, usually parallel to the length of the crystals; uneven fracture.

Allanite (Orthite)

$(Ca,Ce,Y,La,Th)_2(Al,Fe)_3Si_3O_{12}(OH)$ Monoclinic. Commonly metamict, as a result of radiation damage caused by radioactive decay of thorium. **Habit** Crystals usually tabular, long prismatic to acicular; commonly compact massive. **Colour** Usually black, sometimes light to dark brown. Vitreous lustre, sometimes pitchy. Grey-brown streak. **Occurrence** Found as a widespread accessory mineral in many granites, and pegmatites, syenites, gneisses and skarns. **Distinguishing properties** Colour and lustre; S.G. 3·4–4·2 (variable); hardness 5–6½; two poor cleavages; conchoidal to uneven fracture. Often weakly radioactive, the rock matrix around the crystals is often stained black as a result.

Piemontite (Piedmontite)

$Ca_2(Al,Fe,Mn)_3Si_3O_{12}(OH)$ Monoclinic **Habit** Crystals usually prismatic or acicular; commonly massive. Twinning is lamellar, but not common. **Colour** Red, reddish-brown to reddish-black; transparent to nearly opaque. Vitreous lustre. **Occurrence** A rare mineral, found in some low-grade schists, and also in metasomatic manganese-ore deposits. **Distinguishing properties** Colour; occurrence; S.G. 3·4–3·5; hardness 6; one perfect cleavage; uneven fracture.

Wollastonite

$CaSiO_3$ Triclinic **Habit** Crystals tabular or short prismatic; usually fibrous masses, sometimes granular and compact. Twinning is common. **Colour** White to grey; transparent to translucent. Vitreous lustre, somewhat silky in fibrous varieties. White streak. **Occurrence** Formed by the metamorphism of siliceous limestones, both in contact aureoles or in high-grade regionally metamorphosed rocks, usually associated with calcite, epidote, grossular and tremolite. **Distinguishing properties** Habit; colour; association; S.G. 2.8–3·1; hardness $4\frac{1}{2}$–5; one perfect, two other good cleavages; splintery fracture. Dissolves in hydrochloric acid with separation of silica.

Pectolite

NaCa$_2$Si$_3$O$_8$OH Triclinic **Habit** As aggregates of fibrous or acicular crystals; usually radiating and forming globular masses. **Colour** Colourless, white; transparent to translucent. Vitreous or silky lustre. White streak. **Occurrence** Chiefly found in cavities in basaltic rocks, often in association with zeolites; less commonly in calcium-rich metamorphic rocks, also in some alkaline igneous rocks. **Distinguishing properties** The globular aggregates and radiating structures on fracture surfaces are characteristic; S.G. 2·8–2·9; hardness 4½–5; two perfect cleavages; splintery fracture. Easily fusible. Decomposed by hydrochloric acid.

Benitoite

BaTiSi$_3$O$_9$ Hexagonal **Habit** Crystals are rare, pyramidal or tubular, somewhat triangular in shape. **Colour** Blue, purple, pink or white; transparent to translucent. Vitreous lustre. White streak. **Occurrence** As superb blue crystals in association with neptunite and natrolite on serpentine from localities in San Benito County California, United States. Also rarely occurs as detrital grains. **Distinguishing properties** Triangular habit; colour and association with white natrolite and black neptunite are characteristic. S.G. 3·6; hardness 6–6½; indistinct cleavage; conchoidal to uneven fracture. Fluoresces under short-wave ultraviolet light.

Beryl

$Be_3Al_2Si_6O_{18}$ Hexagonal   **Habit**
Crystals are usually short to long
prismatic, faces often striated parallel to
their length and etched.   **Colour**
Commonly pale green, white or yellow;
translucent. Gem varieties are transparent, light to dark green (emerald),
pale blue or green (aquamarine),
yellow (heliodor), pink (morganite).
Vitreous lustre. White streak. **Occurrence** Chiefly as an accessory mineral
in granite and granite-pegmatites in
which crystals often grow to a very
large size. Also found in some biotite
schists, gneisses and pneumatolytic
hydrothermal veins.   **Distinguishing
properties** Hexagonal crystal form;
colour; S.G. 2·6–2·8 (used to distinguish from quartz when massive
white beryl); hardness $7\frac{1}{2}$–8 (compare
apatite) poor basal cleavage; conchoidal to uneven fracture.

Cordierite

$(Mg,Fe)_2Al_4Si_5O_{18}$ Orthorhombic
Habit Rarely as prismatic or pseudo-
hexagonal twinned crystals; generally
massive or irregular grains. Twinning is
common, usually repeated forming
pseudohexagonal crystals.   **Colour**
Dark blue-violet, greyish-blue, also
colourless, yellow, grey or brown;
transparent to translucent. Vitreous
lustre. White streak.   **Occurrence**
Formed by medium- to high-grade
metamorphism of aluminium-rich
rocks. Commonly found in hornfels,
schists and gneisses. **Distinguishing
properties** Colour; granular, colourless
or grey cordierite resembles quartz and
has to be identified by optical or
chemical tests. The gem variety (iolite)
is recognized by its intense pleochroism
(deep blue to yellow); S.G. 2·5–2·8
(increasing with iron content); hardness 7–$7\frac{1}{2}$; one poor cleavage; subconchoidal fracture.

Dioptase

$CuSiO_2(OH)_2$ Hexagonal (Trigonal) **Habit** Crystals short to long prismatic, often terminated by rhombohedra; also massive. **Colour** Emerald-green; transparent to translucent. Vitreous lustre. Pale greenish-blue streak. **Occurrence** Not common but occasionally found in the oxidized zone of copper deposits, sometimes as well-developed crystals associated with other copper minerals and calcite. **Distinguishing properties** The colour of dioptase distinguishes it from other minerals found in copper deposits. S.G. 3·3; hardness 5; perfect rhombohedral cleavage; conchoidal to uneven fracture.

Pyroxene Group

The pyroxenes are a widely distributed group of rock-forming silicates. They have a general formula $X_2Si_2O_6$ and are characterized by two cleavages which intersect almost at right angles.

Orthopyroxenes

Enstatitie and Hypersthene

$MgSiO_3$ and $(Mg,Fe)SiO_3$ Orthorhombic **Habit** Crystals prismatic; usually as grains or massive. **Colour** Pale green to dark brownish-green-black (darkening with Fe). Bronzite is intermediate between enstatite and hypersthene, having a bronzy lustre; translucent to nearly opaque. Vitreous or pearly lustre. White to grey streak. **Occurrence** Found in basic and ultrabasic rocks poor in calcium such as pyroxenites, peridotites and norites. Also in some high-grade metamorphic rocks. **Distinguishing properties** Colour; S.G. 3·4–4·0; (increasing with Fe); hardness 5–6; good prismatic cleavage; uneven fracture.

Clinopyroxenes

Diopside-Hedenbergite-Augite Series

$Ca(Mg,Fe)Si_2O_6$; $Ca(Mg,Fe,Al)$ $(Al,Si)_2O_6$ Monoclinic. These minerals form a continuous series, of which augite is the most common. **Habit** Crystals are usually stout prisms of square or octagonal cross-section; also massive, granular. Twinning is common. **Colour** Dark green to black (augite); greyish white to light green (diopside); translucent to opaque, rarely transparent. Vitreous lustre. White or grey streak. **Occurrence** Augite is abundant in basic and ultrabasic rocks, characteristic of gabbros and basalts. Diopside and hedenbergite occur in medium- and high-grade metamorphic rocks especially those rich in calcium. Light green diopside occurs commonly in metamorphosed dolomite limestones. **Distinguishing properties** Habit; S.G. $3 \cdot 2 - 3 \cdot 6$ (increasing with Fe); hardness $5\frac{1}{2} - 6\frac{1}{2}$; good prismatic cleavage, sometimes well developed basal parting.

Jadeite

$NaAlSi_2O_6$ Monoclinic **Habit** Crystals are very rare; normally found as fine granular or dense masses. **Colour** Various shades of light or dark green, sometimes white or lilac; translucent. Vitreous lustre, perhaps pearly. White streak. **Occurrence** Formed at high pressures and occurs in metamorphosed sodic sediments and volcanic rocks often associated with the amphibole-glaucophane group. Found also as discrete grains. Twinning is sociated with serpentine. **Distinguishing properties** Habit; colour; S.G. $3 \cdot 2 - 3 \cdot 4$; hardness $6 - 6\frac{1}{2}$; good prismatic cleavage; fine grained massive material extremely tough; splintery fracture. The name 'jade' used for the semi-precious stone is applied to two distinct minerals, jadeite and nephrite (an amphibole).

Aegirine

$NaFeSi_2O_6$ Monoclinic A solid solution series exists between aegirine and augite. **Habit** Usually as slender prismatic crystals, often elongated and terminated by steeply inclined faces giving a pointed appearance (acmite); also as discrete grains. Twinning is common. **Colour** Usually dark green to black; subtransparent to opaque. Vitreous lustre. Grey streak. **Occurrence** Found in sodium-rich igneous rocks, especially in nepheline syenites and associated pegmatites. **Distinguishing properties** Habit; association; S.G. 3·5–3·6; hardness 6; good prismatic cleavage; uneven fracture.

Spodumene

$LiAlSi_2O_6$ Monoclinic **Habit** Crystals usually prismatic or lath-like, often striated along their length also massive and columnar, etched and corroded. Twinning is common. **Colour** Commonly white or grey; some varieties are transparent, pink-violet (kunzite) or green (hiddenite) resulting from the presence of small quantities of chromium; translucent. Vitreous lustre. White streak. **Occurrence** Found typically in lithium-bearing granite pegmatites associated with lepidolite, tourmaline and beryl. **Distinguishing properties** Habit; occurrence and association; S.G. 3·0–3·2; hardness $6\frac{1}{2}$–7; perfect prismatic cleavage, usually with a well-developed parting; uneven splintery fracture. Colours a flame red (lithium). Alters readily to clay minerals.

Amphibole Group

Widely distributed in igneous and metamorphic rocks. The amphibole minerals are characterized by two cleavages intersecting at about 120°. The amphiboles contain essential hydroxyl groups in their structure.

Anthophyllite

$(Mg,Fe)_7Si_8O_{22}(OH)_2$ Orthorhombic **Habit** Individual crystals rare, usually in aggregates of prismatic crystals; sometimes fibrous and asbestiform. **Colour** White, grey or brown; translucent. Vitreous lustre, somewhat silky in fibrous varieties. White streak. **Occurrence** Typically found in medium-grade magnesium-rich metamorphic rocks, often associated with talc or cordierite. **Distinguishing properties** Habit; colour; S.G. 2·9–3·3 (increasing with Fe content); hardness 6; perfect prismatic cleavage.

Cummingtonite

$(Fe,Mg)_7Si_8O_{22}(OH)_2$ Monoclinic. Iron rich varieties of cummingtonite are called grunerite; manganese is sometimes present replacing part of the iron and magnesium. **Habit** Usually in aggregates of fibrous crystals; often radiating. **Colour** Pale to dark brown. Vitreous lustre, fibrous variety, silky. White streak. **Occurrence** Found in calcium-poor, iron-rich medium-grade metamorphic rocks, often in association with ore deposits. Also in some igneous rocks such as rhyolites, and as a replacement product of pyroxenes in diorites. **Distinguishing properties** Colour; S.G. 3·2–3·6 (increasing with Fe content); hardness 6; prismatic, perfect cleavage.

Tremolite-Actinolite

$Ca_2(Mg,Fe)_5Si_8O_{22}(OH)_2$ Monoclinic. Tremolite is the low-iron end of a compositional series and actinolite is the iron-rich member. **Habit** Normally as aggregates of long prismatic crystals; sometimes massive, fibrous. **Colour** White to grey (tremolite) becoming green with increasing iron content. Vitreous lustre. White streak. **Occurrence** Common in low- and medium-grade metamorphic rocks, tremolite being characteristic of thermally metamorphosed dolomite limestones; actinolite generally occurs in schists formed by low-medium grade metamorphism of basic igneous rocks. **Distinguishing properties** Habit; colour; S.G. 2·9–3·4; hardness 5–6; good prismatic cleavage. Does not react with hydrochloric acid.

Glaucophane-Riebeckite Series

$Na_2(Mg,Fe,Al)_5Si_8O_{22}(OH)_2$ Monoclinic **Habit** Well-developed crystals rare; often prismatic or acicular, sometimes fibrous or asbestiform. **Colour** Glaucophane is grey, grey-blue or lavender-blue, riebeckite is dark blue to black; translucent to subtranslucent. Vitreous lustre, silky in fibrous varieties. White to blue-grey streak. **Occurrence** Glaucophane is typically found in sodium-rich schists formed by the low-temperature, high-pressure metamorphism of synclinal sediments, usually associated with jadeite, aragonite, chlorite and garnet. Riebeckite occurs mainly in alkaline igneous rocks such as some granites, or nepheline syenites. Fibrous riebeckite (crocidolite or blue asbestos) occurs in veins in bedded ironstones. **Distinguishing properties** Habit; colour and association; S.G. 3·0–3·4 (increasing with Fe content); hardness 5–6; good prismatic cleavage; uneven fracture.

Hornblende

$(Ca,Na)_{2-3}(Mg,Fe,Al)_5(Si,Al)_8O_{22}(OH)_2$ Monoclinic. Varieties occurring in basic igneous rocks often contain appreciable amounts of titanium (kaersutite), or may be low in hydroxyl (basaltic hornblende). **Habit** Crystals usually short or long prismatic, often with six-sided cross sections; also massive, granular or fibrous. Twinning is common. **Colour** Light green to dark green, nearly black; translucent to nearly opaque. Vitreous lustre. White to grey streak. **Occurrence** Very common rock-forming mineral. A common constituent of granodiorites, diorites, gabbros and their fine-grained equivalents. Also in medium-grade, regionally metamorphosed rocks such as amphibolites and hornblende schists. **Distinguishing properties** Colour; S.G. 3·0–3·5 (increasing with Fe content); hardness 5—6; good prismatic cleavage; uneven fracture.

Rhodonite

$MnSiO_3$ Triclinic **Habit** Crystals uncommon, but prismatic or tabular; most commonly massive or granular. **Colour** Pink to rose-red, often veined by black manganese alteration products; transparent to translucent. Vitreous lustre. White streak. **Occurrence** Commonly found associated with manganese-ore deposits either as hydrothermal or metasomatic veins; occurs in some metamorphosed manganese-bearing sediments. **Distinguishing properties** Colour; S.G. 3·5–3·7; hardness $5\frac{1}{2}$–$6\frac{1}{2}$; two perfect and good basal cleavages, conchoidal to uneven fracture. Does not effervesce with warm hydrochloric acid.

Mica Group

The micas constitute an isomorphous group with a general formula of $W(X,Y)_{2-3}Z_4O_{10}(OH,F)_2$. In this W is generally potassium, X and Y can be aluminium, magnesium, iron and lithium, and Z is silicon and aluminium.

Muscovite

$KAl_2(AlSi_3O_{10})(OH)_2$ Monoclinic
Habit Crystals tabular and hexagonal in outline; usually as lamellar masses or small flakes. **Colour** Colourless, or pale shades of green, grey or brown; transparent to translucent. Vitreous lustre; pearly parallel to cleavage. White streak. **Occurrence** Very common in alkali granites and pegmatites. Also common in schists and gneisses of low-medium grade metamorphism. Often found as flakes in sandstones and siltstones. **Distinguishing properties** Habit; S.G. 2·8–2·9; Hardness $2\frac{1}{2}$–4; perfect basal cleavage; cleavage flakes are flexible and elastic.

Biotite and Phlogopite

$K(Mg,Fe)_3AlSi_3O_{10}(OH)_2$ and
$K.Mg_3AlSi_3O_{10}(OH)_2$ Monoclinic
Habit Crystals tabular or short pseudo-hexagonal prisms; also as lamellar aggregates or disseminated flakes. **Colour** Phlogopite, pale yellow to brown, often with a distinctive coppery appearance; biotite, black, dark brown or greenish-black; transparent to translucent. Vitreous lustre, pearly on cleavage surfaces. White or grey streak. **Occurrence** Phlogopite is most commonly found in metamorphosed limestones and in magnesium-rich igneous rocks. Biotite is widely distributed in granite, diorite and syenite, and mica lamprophyres. Commonly found in metamorphic schists and gneisses. **Distinguishing properties** Colour; S.G. 2·7–3·4 (increasing with iron content); hardness 2–3; perfect basal cleavage.

Lepidolite

$K(Li,Al)_3(Si,Al)_4O_{10}(OH)_2$ Monoclinic
Habit Crystals tabular, pseudo-hexagonal; usually as small disseminated flakes. **Colour** Commonly pale lilac, also colourless, pale yellow or grey; transparent to translucent. Vitreous lustre, pearly on cleavage surfaces. **Occurrence** Found in granite pegmatites, often in association with lithium-bearing tourmaline and spodumene. The mineral is mined as a source of lithium compounds. **Distinguishing properties** Habit and colour; S.G. 2·8–3·3; hardness $2\frac{1}{2}$–3; perfect basal cleavage, giving flexible and elastic flakes.

Vermiculite (illustrated)

$Mg_3(Al,Si)_4O_{10}(OH)_2.4H_2O$ Monoclinic **Habit** As platy crystals. **Colour** Yellow, brown; translucent. Pearly lustre, often bronzy. White streak. **Occurrence** Found as an alteration product of magnesium micas, often in association with carbonatites. **Distinguishing properties** Habit and colour; S.G. about 2·3; hardness about $1\frac{1}{2}$. On heating, vermiculite expands greatly perpendicular to cleavage.

Illite

Monoclinic. An aluminosilicate of potassium structurally related to the micas. **Habit** Massive and fine-grained. **Colour** White or other pale colour. **Occurrence** A clay mineral present in shales and sediments. Also as a hydrothermal mineral. **Distinguishing properties** S.G. 2·6–2·9; hardness 1–2; association.

Glauconite (illustrated)

$K(Fe,Mg,Al)_2(Si_4O_{10})(OH)_2$ Monoclinic **Habit** As small, rounded aggregates. **Colour** Green to black, often weathers brown. Earthy and dull lustre. Green streak. **Occurrence** Formed usually in marine sedimentary rocks. The related mineral species, celadonite, is similar in structure and composition to glauconite, but is formed as a blue-green earthy material in vesicular cavities in basalts. **Distinguishing properties** Habit and colour; S.G. 2·5–2·8; hardness 2; perfect basal cleavage.

Sepiolite

$Mg_2(Si_3O_6)(OH)_4$ Monoclinic **Habit** Compact mineral with soft, earthy texture. **Colour** White or other pale shades; opaque. **Occurrence** A secondary mineral often associated with serpentine. **Distinguishing properties** S.G. 2; hardness 2–2½.

Talc (Steatite, Soapstone)

$Mg_3Si_4O_{10}(OH)_2$ Monoclinic **Habit** Crystals are rare; usually as granular or foliated masses. **Colour** White, grey or pale green, often stained reddish; translucent. Dull lustre, pearly on cleavage surfaces. White to pale-green streak. **Occurrence** Found as a secondary mineral formed as a result of the alteration of olivine, pyroxene and amphibole, often lining faults in basic rocks. Also found in low-medium grade metamorphic rocks formed from magnesium-rich rocks, often associated with actinolite. Sometimes formed as a result of the thermal metamorphism of dolomite limestones. **Distinguishing properties** Habit; colour; S.G. 2·6–2·8; hardness 1 (extreme softness); soapy feel; perfect basal cleavage.

Chlorite Group

$(Mg,Fe,Al)_6(Al,Si)_4O_{10}(OH)_8$ Monoclinic **Habit** Crystals are tabular often pseudohexagonal, rarely prismatic; also as scaly aggregates, and massive, earthy. **Colour** Usually green; manganese varieties are orange-brown; chromium-bearing varieties, violet. Vitreous to earthy lustre. White, pale-green streak. **Occurrence** Often found in igneous rocks as an alteration product of pyroxenes, amphiboles and micas. In lavas, infilling amygdales. It is a characteristic mineral of low-grade metamorphic rocks, and is present in the clay mineral fraction of many sediments. Chamosite is an iron-rich chlorite important as a constituent of some sedimentary iron ores. **Distinguishing properties** Habit; colour; S.G. 2·6–3·3 (increasing with Fe content); hardness 2–3; perfect basal cleavage, flakes flexible but not elastic.

Kaolinite

$Al_2Si_2O_5(OH)_4$ Triclinic **Habit** As microscopic pseudohexagonal platy crystals; usually in earthy aggregates. **Colour** White, sometimes stained brown or grey. Dull lustre, crystalline plates pearly. White streak. **Occurrence** A secondary mineral produced by the alteration of aluminous silicates especially the alkali feldspars. **Distinguishing properties** S.G. 2·6–2·7; hardness 2–2½; perfect basal cleavage; plastic feel. For positive identification from other clay minerals, chemical and optical tests must be made. Dickite, nacrite and halloysite are minerals similar in composition to kaolinite. X-ray is usually required for positive identification.

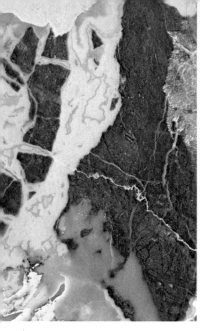

Serpentine Group

$Mg_3Si_2O_5(OH)_4$ Monoclinic. Serpentine, applies to material containing one or more of the minerals chrysotile, antigorite, and lizardite. **Habit** Antigorite generally has a lamellar or platy structure; crystals virtually unknown. Chrysotile is fibrous. **Colour** Various shades of green, also brownish; translucent to opaque. Waxy or greasy lustre in massive varieties, silky in fibrous material. White streak. **Occurrence** Formed by the alteration of olivine and enstatite under conditions of low- to medium-grade metamorphism. Found typically in serpentinites which have formed from the alteration of olivine-rich rocks. **Distinguishing properties** Habit (chrysotile); colour; lustre; smooth rather greasy feel; S.G. 2·5–2·6; hardness, variable $2\frac{1}{2}$–4; perfect basal cleavage (antigorite and lizardite), none in fibrous chrysotile.

Apophyllite

$KCa_4Si_8O_{20}(F,OH).8H_2O$ Tetragonal **Habit** Well-developed crystals of varied habit, usually as combinations of prism, bipyramid and pinacoid. **Colour** Colourless white or grey, sometimes pink to yellow; transparent to translucent. Pearly lustre parallel to basal cleavage, vitreous elsewhere. White streak. **Occurrence** Occurs in association with zeolites in cavities in basalt, commonly associated with prehnite, analcime, stilbite and calcite. Found less commonly in cavities in some granite, gneiss and limestones. Also occurs in some hydrothermal mineral veins. **Distinguishing properties** The basal pinacoid faces are often rough and pitted. Lustre; S.G. 2·3–2·4; hardness $4\frac{1}{2}$–5; perfect basal, poor prismatic cleavages; uneven fracture.

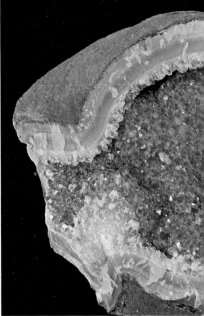

Silica Group

Includes those minerals whose composition is, SiO_2.

Quartz

SiO_2 Hexagonal (Trigonal) **Habit** Crystals are usually six-sided prisms, terminated by six faces, (two sets of rhombohedrons), prism faces may be striated at right angles to the length of the crystal. Shapes range from very elongated to equant. also massive. Most crystals are twinned, but this may be difficult to detect; the three common types are Dauphiné, the Brazil (penetration twins) and the Japan (contact twin). **Colour** Usually colourless (rock crystal) or white. Coloured varieties are often used as semi-precious stones: amethyst-purple; rose-quartz-pink; citrine-yellow brown; smoky quartz-brown to almost black; milky quartz-white. Some quartz varieties contain impurities — such as hair-like inclusions of rutile (rutilated quartz). Ferruginous quartz is a brick red or yellow. Opaque, 'tiger-eye',

compact is quartz that has replaced fibrous asbestos fibres. Aventurine is a variety containing brilliant scales of hematite or mica; transparent to translucent. Vitreous lustre. White streak. **Occurrence** Abundant, occurring in most igneous metamorphic and sedimentary rocks, sometimes composing almost all of the rock, as in quartzites (metamorphic) and some sandstones (sedimentary). Also as a gangue mineral in mineral veins. Well-formed crystal groups are often obtained from geodes in granite pegmatites. Quartz exists in two modifications depending on the temperature of formation. **Distinguishing properties** Habit; S.G. 2·65; hardness 7; conchoidal fracture. Usually fresh and unaltered. Not attacked by acids, other than hydrofluoric.

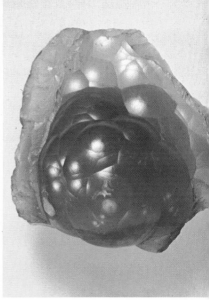

Quartz (variety Chalcedony)

SiO_2 Chalcedony is the name given to compact varieties of silica which are formed of quartz crystallites often fibrous in form and with sub-microscopic pores. **Habit** Massive, as mamillated, botryoidal or stalactitic forms. **Colour** Chalcedony is distinguished from agate by its lack of obvious colour banding, but exhibits the same range of colours: colourless to white, grey, red, brown, green or yellow. Some coloured varieties have various names: carnelian-red, sard-brown, chrysoprase-apple-green, heliotrope (bloodstone)-green with spots of red jasper; transparent to translucent. Jasper is opaque chalcedony and generally red but also yellow, brown and green varieties occur. Colour is often distributed in spots or bands. Vitreous to waxy lustre. **Occurrence** Found lining or filling cavities or fissures in rocks having been deposited from silica-rich aqueous solutions, usually formed at low to moderate temperatures by the crystallization of originally colloidal material. Chert and flint occur as dark nodules or thin beds in sedimentary rocks and originate either by the deposition of silica on the sea floor, or by the replacement of rocks, notably limestones, or by silica from percolating waters. **Distinguishing properties** Habit; colour; occurrence; S.G. about 2·6; hardness about $6\frac{1}{2}$; conchoidal fracture.

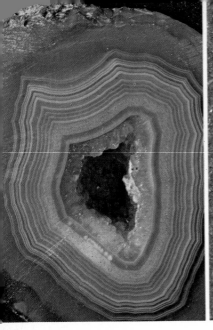 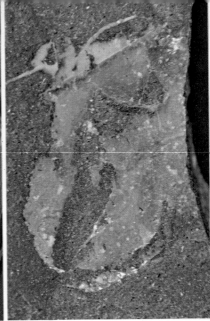

Quartz (variety Agate)

SiO_2 **Habit** Usually found as concentric or irregular layers lining a cavity, which may be partially or completely filled by quartz crystals. **Colour** The bands are usually variegated in shades of white, grey, green, brown, red or black. Commercial agate is often coloured artificially. Parallel banded agate in shades of white with black, brown or brownish red, is named onyx and sardonyx. Moss agate contains mineral impurities such as manganese oxides and chlorite in moss-like patterns. **Occurrence** Typically found in volcanic lavas as a cavity filling from silica-rich solutions. The colour banding may be due to slight changes in the composition of the solutions due to changing physical conditions. **Distinguishing properties** Habit; S.G. about 2·6; hardness about $6\frac{1}{2}$; conchoidal fracture.

Opal

$SiO_2.nH_2O$ Amorphous. Opal is a hydrous submicrocrystalline form of cristobalite. **Habit** Massive; as veinlets, stalactitic or botryoidal. Often replaces other substances such as wood (wood opal). **Colour** Colourless, grey, red, brown and blue-green. Precious opal is milky-white, sometimes black, exhibiting a play of colours due to the internal structure; red and yellow are dominant in fire opal. Common opal is translucent, lacking a play of colours; transparent to translucent. Vitreous often resinous lustre. **Occurrence** Found filling and lining cavities in igneous and sedimentary rocks, especially in areas of hot springs. Often forms skeletons of organisms, e.g. sponges, accumulating to form a fine-grained sedimentary rock (diatomaceous earth). **Distinguishing properties** Lustre; S.G. variable, 1·8–2·3; hardness $5\frac{1}{2}$–$6\frac{1}{2}$; conchoidal fracture.

Feldspar Group

The feldspars are the most abundant of all minerals being widely distributed in igneous, metamorphic and sedimentary rocks. The general formula is $X(Al,Si)_4O_8$, X is Na,K,Ca or Ba.

Potassic Feldspars

Microcline

$KAlSi_3O_8$ Triclinic **Habit** Usually short prismatic. Simple twins, but shows repeated twinning. **Colour** White, cream, pink; sometimes green (amazonstone); translucent to subtranslucent. Vitreous lustre, sometimes pearly on cleavage surfaces. White streak. **Occurrence** Usually forms at lower temperatures than orthoclase and is the common potassic feldspar in pegmatites and hydrothermal veins. Also occurs in some metamorphic rocks. **Distinguishing properties** From orthoclase only by optical properties. S.G. 2·5–2·6; hardness 6; two good cleavages; conchoidal to uneven fracture.

Orthoclase and Sanidine

$KAlSi_3O_8$ Monoclinic **Habit** Crystals usually prismatic; may be with square cross-section, sometimes flattened or tabular (sanidine). Twinning is common. **Colour** Sanidine is colourless to grey; transparent. Orthoclase is white to flesh-pink, occasionally red; translucent to subtranslucent. Vitreous lustre, sometimes pearly on cleavage surfaces. White streak. **Occurrence** Sanidine is the high-temperature form and it occurs as phenocrysts in volcanic rocks; also in metamorphic rocks. Orthoclase is the common potassic feldspar of most igneous and metamorphic rocks. Also occurs as perthitic intergrowth with albite. **Distinguishing features** Sanidine and orthoclase can be distinguished from the plagioclase feldspars by the absence of twinning striations. S.G. 2·5–2·6; hardness 6–$6\frac{1}{2}$; two perfect cleavages; conchoidal to uneven fracture.

 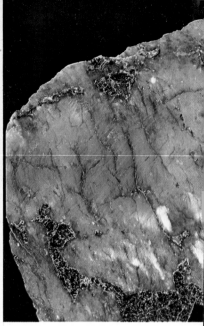

Adularia

KAlSi$_3$O$_8$ Monoclinic **Habit** Occurs as distinctive simple crystals, usually a combination of prisms terminated by two faces, which often have the appearance of rhombohedra. Twinning is common. **Colour** Colourless or milky white, often with a pearly sheen or play of colours (moonstones); transparent to translucent. Vitreous lustre. White streak. **Occurrence** Formed at low temperatures and is found in hydrothermal veins. **Distinguishing properties** Habit and occurrence; S.G. 2·6; hardness 6; two perfect cleavages; conchoidal to uneven fracture.

Plagioclase Feldspars

NaAlSi$_3$O$_8$CaAl$_2$Si$_2$O$_8$ Triclinic. The composition changes progressively from albite (NaAlSi$_3$O$_8$) (illustrated) through oligoclase — andesine-labradorite-bytownite to anorthite (CaAl$_2$Si$_2$O$_8$). **Habit** Crystals prismatic or tabular; also massive, granular. Repeated twinning is common on albite and pericline laws and shows as a series of parallel striations, also simple twins, on Carlsbad, Baveno and Manebach laws. **Colour** Usually white or off-white, sometimes pink, greenish or brownish; transparent to translucent. Vitreous lustre, sometimes pearly on cleavage surfaces. White streak. **Occurrence** The plagioclase feldspars occur in many igneous rocks and are used as a basis of igneous rock classification. In general the sodic plagioclases are found in granite igneous rocks and calcic plagioclases in basalts and gabbros. Between potassic feldspar and albite there exists a continuous series as sodium substitutes for potassium; this series is

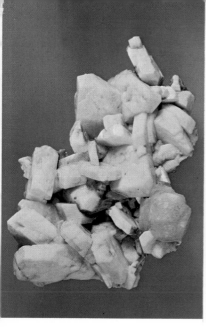

called the alkali feldspar series. Anorthosites are rocks formed almost completely of oligoclase-andesine plagioclase feldspar. Albite is commonly found in pegmatites and in sodic lavas. Plagioclase is also common in metamorphic rocks and as detrital grains. **Distinguishing properties** Repeated twin lamellae. Labradorite cleavages commonly show a play of colours in shades of blue and green (illustrated). S.G. 2·6–2·8; hardness 6–6½; two good cleavages; uneven fracture.

Feldspathoid Group

Feldspathoid minerals are a group of sodium and potassium aluminosilicates which are formed in place of feldspars when an alkali-rich magma is deficient in silica.

Nepheline

$NaAlSiO_4$ Hexagonal **Habit** Crystals are usually six-sided prisms, commonly found as shapeless or irregular grains. **Colour** Usually colourless, white or grey but also brownish-red or greenish; transparent to translucent. Vitreous to greasy lustre. White streak. **Occurrence** Characteristic mineral of silica-poor alkali igneous rocks of both plutonic and volcanic associations. **Distinguishing properties** Habit; lustre; S.G. 2·6–2·7; hardness 5½–6; indistinct prismatic and basal cleavages; conchoidal fracture. Readily decomposed by hydrochloric acid.

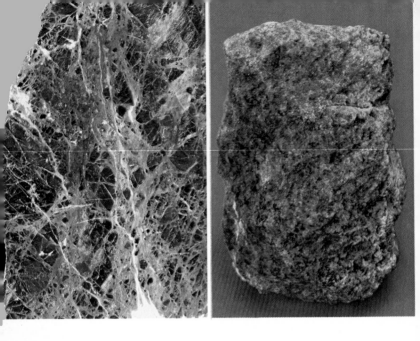

Sodalite

$Na_8Al_6Si_6O_{24}Cl_2$ Cubic **Habit** Crystals are rare, sometimes as small dodecahedral crystals; commonly massive and granular. **Colour** Commonly azure-blue, also pink, yellow, green or grey-white; transparent to translucent. Vitreous lustre. White streak. **Occurrence** Often found associated with nepheline in alkali igneous rocks such as nepheline-syenites, also in some silica-poor dyke rocks and lavas. **Distinguishing properties** Colour; S.G. 2·3; hardness $5\frac{1}{2}$–6; poor dodecahedral cleavage; uneven to conchoidal fracture. Distinguished from lazurite by its occurrence and by the absence of associated pyrite. Often shows reddish flourescence in ultraviolet light. Gelatinizes in hydrochloric acid.

Hauyne (illustrated) and Nosean

$(Na,Ca)_{4-8}Al_6Si_6O_{24}(SO_4)_{1-2}$ and $Na_8Al_6(SiO_4)_6SO_4$ Cubic **Habit** Crystals usually dodecahedral or octahedral; commonly as rounded grains. Twinning is common; sometimes as penetration twins. **Colour** Often blue, also grey, brown, yellow-green; transparent to translucent. Vitreous to greasy lustre. White streak. **Occurrence** Found in silica-poor lavas such as phonolites and related igneous rocks in association with leucite or nepheline. **Distinguishing properties** Colour, association; S.G. (hauyne) 2·4–2·5, (nosean) 2·3–2·4; hardness $5\frac{1}{2}$–6; poor dodecahedral cleavage; uneven to conchoidal fracture.

Lazurite

$(Na,Ca)_8(Al,Si)_{12}O_{24}(S,SO_4)$ Cubic. Lazurite is isomorphous with sodalite but has sulphide ions in place of chloride ions. **Habit** Crystals rare; usually as cubes or dodecahedra. **Colour** Azure-blue; translucent. Vitreous lustre. Bright-blue streak. **Occurrence** A rare mineral, usually occurring in crystalline limestones as a product of contact metamorphism. Often in association with calcite and enclosing small grains of pyrite. Lapis lazuli is a rock rich in lazurite and is used as a decorative stone. **Distinguishing properties** Colour; association with calcite and pyrite; S.G. 2·4; hardness 5–5½; imperfect dodecahedral cleavage. Soluble in hydrochloric acid.

Scapolite

$(Na,Ca,K)_4Al_3(Al,Si)_3Si_6O_{24}(Cl,F,OH, CO_3,SO_4)$ Tetragonal. Scapolites vary between a sodic-end member (marialite) and a calcic-end member (meionite). **Habit** Crystals usually prismatic, often with uneven faces; mostly massive or granular. **Colour** Usually white or grey, sometimes pink, yellow or brownish; transparent to translucent. Vitreous to pearly lustre. White streak. **Occurrence** Found typically in metamorphosed limestones, occurs in skarns close to igneous contacts, and in schists and gneisses sometimes replacing plagioclase. **Distinguishing properties** Massive blocky habit; colour; S.G. 2·5–2·8 (increasing with calcium content); hardness 5–6; good prismatic cleavages, these impart a splintery appearance to massive scapolite; subconchoidal fracture.

Leucite

$KAlSi_2O_6$ Tetragonal (pseudocubic). Leucite is tetragonal, pseudocubic at ordinary temperatures; cubic above 625°C. **Habit** Crystals nearly always icositetrahedra. **Colour** Usually white or grey; translucent. Vitreous lustre. White streak. **Occurrence** Found typically embedded in potassium-rich silica-poor lavas such as trachytes. Does not occur in plutonic igneous rocks. **Distinguishing properties** Crystal form and occurrence. Analcime also crystallizes as icositetrahedra but occurs typically in cavities, not as embedded crystals. S.G. 2·5; hardness 5½–6; very poor cleavage; conchoidal fracture. Leucite often alters to pseudoleucite, a pseudomorph consisting of nepheline, analcime and orthoclase. Infusible.

Zeolite Group

Zeolites are hydrated alumino-silicates, chiefly of Na and Ca, less commonly K, Ba, and Sr. They are not related in crystal structure but have a structure enclosing pores occupied by water molecules that can be continuously expelled on heating.

Analcime (Analcite)

$NaAlSi_2O_6.H_2O$ Cubic **Habit** Usually icositetrahedral; also granular and massive. **Colour** Colourless, white or grey, often tinged with pink, yellow or green; transparent to translucent. Vitreous lustre. White streak. **Occurrence** Commonly found as a secondary mineral in cavities, in basaltic rocks associated with other zeolites. Also in some sedimentary rocks as a secondary mineral. Occasionally as a primary mineral in silica-deficient igneous rocks. **Distinguishing properties** Crystal form; mode of occurrence; S.G. 2·2–2·3; hardness 5–5½; very poor cubic cleavage; subconchoidal fracture.

Chabazite

$CaAl_2Si_4O_{12}.6H_2O$ Hexagonal (Trigonal) **Habit** Usually occurs as simple rhombohedral crystals which look like cubes. Penetration twins common. **Colour** Usually white, yellow, often pinkish or red; transparent to translucent. Vitreous lustre. White streak. **Occurrence** Typically occurs lining cavities in basalts and andesites, associated with other zeolites. **Distinguishing properties** Crystal form; S.G. 2·0–2·1; hardness 4–5; poor rhombohedral cleavage; uneven fracture. Does not effervesce in acid.

Natrolite

$Na_2Al_2Si_3O_{10}.2H_2O$ Orthorhombic (pseudotetragonal) **Habit** Usually as prismatic crystals, commonly elongated and needle-like; frequently as divergent or radiating aggregates. Also as compact masses. **Colour** Colourless to white, grey yellow or red; transparent to translucent. Vitreous lustre. White streak. **Occurrence** Typically occurs as crystals lining cavities in basaltic rocks. **Distinguishing properties** Habit; S.G. 2·2–2·3; hardness 5–5$\frac{1}{2}$; perfect prismatic cleavage. Mesolite and scolecite are also fibrous zeolites of similar composition and occurrence to natrolite, they are both monoclinic and fibrous; optical or X-ray tests are needed for positive identification.

Thomsonite

$NaCa_2(Al,Si)_{10}O_{20}.6H_2O$ Orthorhombic (pseudotetragonal) **Habit** Usually as acicular crystals in radiating or divergent aggregates. **Colour** White, sometimes tinged with red; transparent to translucent. Vitreous to pearly lustre. White streak. **Occurrence** Associated with other zeolites, in cavities in basalts and related igneous rocks. Also found as an alteration product of nepheline. **Distinguishing properties** Slightly more coarsely crystalline than natrolite. S.G. 2·1–2·4; hardness 5–5$\frac{1}{2}$; two good cleavages; uneven fracture.

Laumontite

$CaAl_2Si_4O_{12}.4H_2O$ Monoclinic **Habit** Commonly as small prismatic crystals often with oblique terminations; also massive, or as columnar and radiating aggregates. Frequently twinned, sometimes as 'swallow-tail' twins. **Colour** White, sometimes reddish; transparent to translucent. Vitreous lustre, pearly on cleavage surfaces. White streak. **Occurrence** Occurs with other zeolites in veins and amygdales in igneous rocks. It is also produced as a result of very low-grade metamorphism of some sedimentary rocks and tuffs. **Distinguishing properties** Habit; S.G. 2·2–2·4; hardness 3–4; two perfect cleavages; uneven fracture. Characteristic alteration, laumonite loses part of its water on exposure to dry air and becomes powdery, friable and chalky (variety leonhardite).

Heulandite

$(Ca, Na_2)Al_2Si_7O_{18}.6H_2O$ Monoclinic
Habit Crystals are usually tabular, 'coffin-shaped', often in subparallel aggregates; also massive, granular. **Colour** Colourless, white, grey, pink, red or brown; transparent to translucent. Vitreous lustre, pearly on cleavage surfaces. White streak. **Occurrence** A common zeolite mineral, often associated with stilbite in cavities in basaltic rocks, and sometimes found in sedimentary rocks as a secondary mineral. **Distinguishing properties** Habit; lustre; S.G. 2·1–2·2; hardness $3\frac{1}{2}$–4; one perfect cleavage; uneven fracture.

Stilbite

$NaCa_2Al_5Si_{13}O_{36}.14H_2O$ Monoclinic
Habit Commonly found as sheaf-like aggregates formed by cruciform penetration twins; also massive or globular. Twinning is common, forming cruciform interpenetrant twins. **Colour** White sometimes yellowish or pink, occasionally brick-red; transparent to translucent. Vitreous lustre, pearly on cleavage surfaces. White streak. **Occurrence** Found in cavities in basalts, commonly in association with heulandite. **Distinguishing properties** Habit; lustre; S.G. 2·1–2·2; hardness $3\frac{1}{2}$–4; one perfect cleavage; uneven fracture.

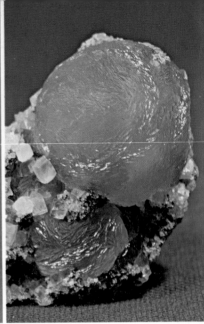

Petalite

$LiAlSi_4O_{10}$ Monoclinic **Habit** Crystals are well-formed but small; usually as large cleavable, blocky masses. Polysynthetic twinning. **Colour** Colourless, white, grey or yellow; transparent to translucent. Vitreous lustre, pearly on cleavages. White streak. **Occurrence** In granite pegmatites in association with cleavelandite, quartz and lepidolite. **Distinguishing properties** Association; S.G. 2·3–2·5; hardness 6–6$\frac{1}{2}$; two good cleavages; subconchoidal fracture.

Prehnite

$Ca_2Al_2Si_3O_{10}(OH)_2$ Orthorhombic **Habit** Crystals rare, commonly tabular; usually massive, botryoidal or stalactitic. **Colour** Characteristically pale green, sometimes white, yellowish or grey. Vitreous to somewhat pearly lustre. White streak. **Occurrence** Occurs chiefly in cavities in basic igneous rocks, often associated with zeolites; also in low-grade metamorphic rocks and as an alteration product in some altered igneous rocks. **Distinguishing properties** Habit; colour; S.G. 2·9–3·0; hardness 6–6$\frac{1}{2}$; good basal cleavage; uneven fracture.

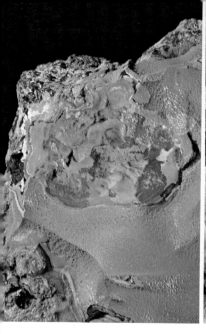

Chrysocolla

near $CuSiO_3.2H_2O$ possibly Orthorhombic **Habit** Finely fibrous or massive, sometimes botryoidal, earthy. **Colour** Various shades of blue, bluegreen to green, sometimes brown to black when impure; translucent to nearly opaque. Vitreous, waxy, or earthy lustre. White streak. **Occurrence** A fairly common mineral in the oxidation zone of some copper deposits. **Distinguishing properties** Habit; colour; occurrence; S.G. variable, 2·0–2·5; hardness 2–4; conchoidal to uneven fracture.

Tourmaline

$Na(Mg,Fe)_3Al_6(BO_3)_3Si_6O_{18}(OH,F)_4$ Hexagonal (Trigonal). Tourmaline is a general group term that is applied to several minerals with similar atomic structure and chemical composition. The most common of these are elbaite $Na(Li,Al)_3Al_6B_3Si_6O_{27}(OH,F)_4$; schorl $Na(Fe,Mn)_3Al_6B_3Si_6O_{27}(OH,F)_4$; and dravite $NaMg_3Al_6B_3Si_6O_{27}(OH,F)_4$. **Habit** Crystals usually prismatic, often with rounded triangular cross-sections; prism faces commonly strongly striated parallel to their length; the two ends of a crystal are often differently terminated. Parallel or radiating crystal groups are common. **Colour** Usually black, especially schorl, also brown dark blue, colourless (iron-free varieties), pink, green and blue. Crystals are commonly colour-zoned; transparent to nearly opaque. Names of coloured varieties: rubellite (pink and red); indicolite (blue); achroite (colourless); siberite (reddish-violet). Vitreous lustre. White streak. **Occurrence** Commonly in granitic peg-

Tourmaline (continued)

matites, or in granites which have been metasomatically altered by boron-rich fluids. Brown magnesium-rich tourmaline is found in metamorphosed limestone. Also found as an accessory mineral in schists and gneisses. **Distinguishing properties** Habit; striations; triangular cross-section; colour; S.G. 3·0–3·2; hardness 7–7½; very poor cleavage; conchoidal to uneven fracture.

Axinite

$(Ca, Mn, Fe, Mg)_3 Al_2 BSi_4 O_{15}(OH)$ Triclinic **Habit** Crystals usually tabular and wedge-shaped with sharp edges; also massive, lamellar or granular. **Colour** Distinctive clove-brown colour, but sometimes yellow, grey or pink; transparent to translucent. Vitreous lustre. White streak. **Occurrence** Commonly found in calcareous rocks that have undergone contact metamorphism and metasomatism. Also occurs in cavities in granites and in some hydrothermal veins. **Distinguishing properties** Crystal form; colour; S.G. 3·3–3·4; hardness 6½–7; one good cleavage; conchoidal fracture.

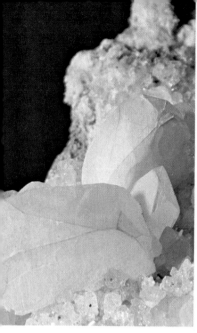

Datolite

CaBSiO$_4$OH Monoclinic **Habit** Usually in short prismatic crystals which often show a variety of forms; or as granular masses. **Colour** Colourless or pale shades of yellow and green, also white; transparent. Vitreous lustre. White streak. **Occurrence** A secondary mineral, usually found in cavities in basic igneous rocks associated with zeolites, prehnites and calcite. Also in some veins and granites. **Distinguishing properties.** Habit; colour; S.G. 2·8–3·0; hardness 5–5$\frac{1}{2}$; uneven to conchoidal fracture.

Dumortierite

Al$_7$O$_3$(BO$_3$)(SiO$_4$)$_3$ Orthorhombic **Habit** Rare as prismatic crystals; usually in fibrous or columnar aggregates; frequently radiating. **Colour** Blue, violet or pink; transparent to translucent. Vitreous or dull lustre. White streak. **Occurrence** Not a common mineral but occurs in considerable amounts at a few localities. Found in some aluminium-rich metamorphic rocks and occasionally in pegmatites. **Distinguishing properties** Habit; colour; S.G. 3·3–3·4; hardness 8$\frac{1}{2}$; one good, one imperfect cleavage.

Further reading

The following publications are recommended for further reading on the study of rocks and minerals or as reference works.

Deer, W.A., Howie, R.A. and Zussman, J., *An introduction to the Rock Forming Minerals*, Longmans, London, 1966.

Ford, W.E., *Dana's Textbook of Mineralogy*, John Wiley, New York, 1932.

Greg, R.P. and Lettsom, W.G., *Mineralogy of Great Britain and Ireland*, 1858. Facsimile reprint, Lapidary Publications, Broadstairs, 1977.

Hamilton, W.R., Woolley, A.R. and Bishop, A.C., *The Hamlyn Guide to Minerals, Rocks and Fossils*, Hamlyn, London, 1974.

Hey, M.H., *Chemical Index of Minerals*, British Museum (Natural History), London, 1955, 1963, 1974.

Kostov, I., *Mineralogy*, Oliver and Boyd, Edinburgh and London, 1968.

Woolley, A.R. (ed.), *The Illustrated Encyclopedia of the Mineral Kingdom*, Hamlyn, London, 1978.

Index

Page numbers shown in italics refer to main descriptions.